DATE DUE

Everyday Life in
Colonial Canada

LORIS RUSSELL

Everyday Life in

COLONIAL CANADA

B. T. BATSFORD

LONDON

Frontispiece: Reaping with cradles

First published 1973
© Loris Russell, 1973

Filmset by Keyspools Ltd, Golborne, Lancashire
Printed in Great Britain by
Fletcher & Sons Ltd, Norwich
for the Publishers
B. T. Batsford, 4 Fitzhardinge Street, London W1H 0AH

ISBN 0 7134 1688 2

Published simultaneously in Canada by
The Copp Clark Publishing Company

ISBN 0 7730 4002 1

CONTENTS

THE ILLUSTRATIONS

ACKNOWLEDGEMENTS

The author wishes to thank the following persons for information supplied and courtesies extended during the preparation of this book: Mr. H. B. Burnham, Mr. D. B. Webster, and Mr. Leigh Warren, Royal Ontario Museum; Brigadier J. A. McGinnis, Toronto Historical Board; Mr. R. K. Cooper and Mr. Harold Lund, Black Creek Pioneer Village; Miss Edith Firth, Metropolitan Toronto Central Library; Mr. F. J. Thorpe, National Museum of Man, Ottawa; Dr. B. Fowler, Ottawa Research Station, Department of Agriculture; Miss M. F. Dissette and Mr. D. R. Hough, Upper Canada Village; Mr. J. D. King, Chateau de Ramezay, Montreal; M. Raymond Gingras, Archives du Québec.

The author and publishers wish to thank the following for permission to reproduce the illustrations listed: Black Creek Pioneer Village (figs. 63, 106, 110); John Robertson Collection, Metropolitan Toronto Central Library (figs. 118, 119); National Museum of Man, National Museums of Canada (frontispiece); Archives of Ontario (figs. 1, 93); Royal Ontario Museum (figs. 39, 40, 89, 100, 103, 117). Photographs not specially credited are by the author.

INTRODUCTION

The colonial period of Canadian history is here taken to be the time between the founding of Quebec in 1608 and the creation of the Dominion of Canada in 1867. During these 259 years Canada changed from a remote outpost of European empire to a potentially independent nation. Along the way there were many changes in national allegiances and political divisions, creating new geographic names or new meanings for old ones.

New France of the seventeenth century consisted of Acadie on the Atlantic and Canada on the St Lawrence River. Acquisition of Acadie by the British in 1713 led to the revival of the old name of Nova Scotia. In 1763 the remaining French possession, Canada, was ceded to Britain. It included not only the St Lawrence settlements, but also the unsettled wilderness westward to Lake Superior. Loss of American colonies in 1783 left Britain with only Newfoundland, Nova Scotia, and Canada, but the influx of the 'United Empire Loyalists', i.e. those Americans who chose to remain British, created the colony of New Brunswick, and the separation of Canada into Lower Canada (the St Lawrence region) and Upper Canada (the Great Lakes region).

Following the rebellion of 1837–38, the two Canadas were united as the Province of Canada in 1840, but the subdivision into Canada East and Canada West was retained for administrative purposes. Later these became the Provinces of Quebec and Ontario.

With the creation of the Dominion of Canada in 1867 the term 'colonial' became unpopular, at least with Canadians, who saw in it a subordinate status, like a daughter still tied to her mother's apron strings. But colonial Canada had seen stirring events and heroic figures, the 'fleurons glorieux' of the song. Their story is indeed a glorious one, but it is not that with which the present study deals. Instead, it is concerned with the thousands of ordinary people who crossed the ocean and penetrated the wilderness to lay the foundations of a future nation. It is with colonials like Louis Hébert, farming the hilltop at Quebec, or Sam Strickland, hacking a home out of the Otanabee bush, or rather what they did and how they did it. What it was like to be a colonial Canadian is the theme of this book.

I

The Settlement

The earliest explorers of America's northern coast were only advance scouts, who left no permanent mark of their presence. Cabot (1497-98) skirted the edges of Newfoundland and Labrador. Cartier (1534-35) touched the shores of the Gaspé Peninsula and penetrated the St Lawrence corridor as far as Montreal ('Hochelaga'), but apart from a tragic wintering at Quebec he made no attempt at settling. Even Port Royal (1605) in the fertile Annapolis Valley of Nova Scotia was only a reconnaissance for the future French settlement of 'La Cadie'. Nor can they be regarded as true settlements, those bases for the fishing fleets along the coasts of Newfoundland and Labrador that according to tradition flourished even before the founding of Quebec.

NEW FRANCE

The first real settlement of the future Canada was that established by Samuel de Champlain, a geographer from Brouage on the Bay of Biscay. He was acting on behalf of a chartered trading organization known as the Company of One Hundred Associates. Champlain built a fort at the base of the Quebec cliffs in 1608. He had been at Port Royal and understood the problems of isolation, frigid winter, and hostile natives. What he was not prepared for was the feeble support of his sponsors and the enmity of the English colonists in the Massachusetts Bay area. But in spite of hardships, lack of support, and even temporary conquest, the settlement at Quebec entrenched itself and became the base for French penetration up the river. A fort was established at the mouth of the St Maurice River in 1634 and named Trois Rivières. A permanent settlement was founded on the Island of Montreal (Ville Marie) in 1642.

The French settlements along the St Lawrence River were

primarily trading posts, where European tools and ornaments were exchanged with the native people for furs, each side being confident that it had got the better of the bargain. But trading establishments had to be fed, and so the cultivation of the land became more and more important. Also, the charter of the Company of One Hundred Associates charged it with the establishment of agricultural settlements. This stipulation was more honoured in the breach, however, and it was not until 1663, when Louis XIV took over direct control of the American colony, that the policy of settlement was vigorously pursued. To help keep the hostile Iroquois in check, soldiers were sent out as settlers; they could farm in periods of peace, and provide trained defence in time of danger. The most famous of such contingents was the Regiment of Carignan-Salière, which had served with distinction in the Thirty Years War. After taking part in a successful campaign against the Iroquois, the regiment was disbanded, and a large number of its members chose to remain in the colony, the officers being granted seigniories, and the men taking up component parts of these grants.

To have a permanent settlement there must be women as well as men. A few of the colonists brought their wives with them, and a few women came out unattached. But this was too slow, so the famous King's Girls were sent out: contingents of young women, mostly from the peasant class, carefully selected for good morals and health, sent overseas at government expense to be chosen as wives by the young men of the colony. Not all the men who came to New France were soldiers. Many came hoping to better themselves in the colony, to have land, and perhaps to rise to a position of importance. Sons of honourable families came to take up seigniories, and to become part of a new landed gentry that contributed much to the development of the colony. Although many parts of France were represented, the great majority of emigrants were from the western provinces, along or near the coast, where the idea of sea voyages and foreign adventure was not strange, even to the peasantry. A strong attraction of the new world was the relative freedom that the colonist enjoyed, far from the absolute rule of monarch and noble in the home land.

In spite of daring explorers, competent soldiers, and zealous missionaries, the colony of New France never expanded much upstream from Montreal. The earliest attempt to establish communities in what is now Ontario was based on the idea of Christianizing and civilizing the Huron Indians, who occupied

the area south-east of Georgian Bay ('Huronia'). This project
came to a disastrous end in 1650 with the destruction of the settlements by Iroquois raiders from south of Lake Ontario. The
calamity seems to have sealed off the west to French settlement,
even though military forts were established along the north shore
of Lake Ontario, and a chain of fur-trading posts was set up
temporarily, perhaps even as far west as the Rocky Mountains.
But by 1763, when Canada was ceded to Britain by the Treaty of
Paris, the only permanent French settlement west of Montreal
was along the Detroit River, which joins Lake St Clair to Lake
Erie.

In the Atlantic region, French settlement spread out from the
foothold at Port Royal. It moved along the Annapolis Valley, and
founded its most prosperous communities at the north-east end,
around Minas Basin. Across the Bay of Fundy, in what is now
New Brunswick, French establishments were set up along the
St Croix River and on the north shore of the bay, but there was
no intensive settlement, as in the Annapolis Valley. France might
have retained possession of these territories had they not been
used for savage raids against the English settlements along the
New England frontier. The aroused British authorities, after
some fumbling, succeeded in capturing Port Royal in 1710, and
as a result all the settlements of 'Acadie' came under British rule.
This was confirmed by the Treaty of Utrecht in 1713, and the
boundary between British and French America became the
Chignecto Isthmus, which joins what are now the Provinces of
Nova Scotia and New Brunswick. The new rulers made no attempt
to interfere with the way of life of the Acadians, as the French
inhabitants were called, only requiring that they take the oath
of allegiance to the British king. Under the influence of the French
across the border, this obligation was ignored. With the outbreak
of the Seven Years War in 1754, British forces seized the French
forts along the frontier. Still the Acadians refused to take the oath
of allegiance, and it was decided that they must go. The melan-
choly story of the expulsion has been told by many historians, but
the best-known version is the semi-fictional poem by Henry
Wadsworth Longfellow, *Evangeline*. A large number of the exiles
found a new home in what is now south-western Louisiana, where
their descendants are still known as 'Cajuns'. But some found
their way back to the shores of Fundy. By this time most of their
homesteads had been taken over by settlers from the English
colonies, so they were forced to look for new homes farther down

the bay, where they created fishing communities along what came to be known as the French Shore.

THE BRITISH COLONIES
English settlement in what was to be Canada began on the Avalon Peninsula of Newfoundland. For many years these establishments were only bases for the rich cod fisheries, and agricultural settlement was far in the future. Rival French settlements in Newfoundland were abandoned under the terms of the Treaty of Utrecht in 1713. But Cape Breton, under the name of Isle Royale, remained under French rule. Meanwhile the Annapolis Valley had been secured by the establishment of Annapolis Royal, near the site of the lost Port Royal. After expulsion of the Acadians from the valley, English colonists, mostly from Massachusetts, moved in, bringing with them the colonial designation of 'planter'. By 1763 most of the land around Minas Basin, so laboriously drained and cultivated by the French, had been taken over by the English-speaking planters, who established a core of British influence that helped to retain Nova Scotia and New Brunswick during the American Revolution.

Across the spine of Nova Scotia on the Atlantic side, a British settlement was established in 1749 at the entrance to the magnificent harbour of Chebucto, which, it was boasted, could hold all the navies of the world. This new centre, really a naval station, was named for the Earl of Halifax. From here, settlement spread up and down the coast, peopled by families from Massachusetts or by disbanded soldiers from British regiments. About 70 miles south-west of Halifax another fine harbour became the port of Lunenburg, established in 1753 by people from Hanover, which was also ruled at that time by the British king.

Lunenburg was the northernmost of the settlements of non-British colonists that were established by a benevolent government in London for continental refugees from persecution, or for those seeking escape from economic depression. When the decision had to be made—Britain or America—many of these people chose to support the régime that had given them freedom and independence. It was ironic that the American Revolution, which began as an armed conflict in 1775, was instigated and led mostly by people of pure English descent, whereas those who remained loyal to British government included a large number of the newer colonists from Germany, the Netherlands, and Switzerland. What was oppression to one group was generous liberalism to the other.

1 Outline map of northern North America, showing (stipple pattern) the maximum extent of New France, about 1700

2 Outline map of North America, showing (stipple pattern) the extent of the British Colonies in 1791, after the American Revolution and the division of the colony of Canada.

THE LOYALISTS

In contrast to the increasing tension in the English-speaking colonies during the 12 years that followed the Treaty of Paris, the newly-acquired French colony of Canada enjoyed a period of tranquillity and prosperity. Retention of language, religion, and seigniorial tenure were permitted by Governors Murray and Carleton and formally guaranteed by the Quebec Act of 1774. Merchants from New York and Boston laid the foundations for the commercial pre-eminence of Montreal. When the test of war came, the French-Canadian clergy and aristocracy supported the English authorities, a small fraction of the townspeople went over to the Americans, and most of the *habitants* remained neutral and aloof. The near success of the American invasion of 1775, accompanied by massive propaganda, made little change in these attitudes. So in the end Quebec remained British. Nova Scotia, too, was saved for the Crown, partly by its remoteness, partly by the hard core of loyal colonists who actively opposed a brief land invasion and a series of petty naval raids from the south. As the probable success of the revolution became evident, the loyal American colonists, through fear or actual threat, began to abandon their homes and to gather in centres where British power was still unshaken. One such place was the town of New York, which drew Loyalists from as far as Massachusetts and Virginia. From northern New England and the Mohawk Valley of New York the loyal colonists gathered around Montreal, many of them taking part in the border skirmishes against those who had driven them from their homes. The second Treaty of Paris in 1783 brought American independence, and the final disinheritance of those who had stood for a 'united empire'. Unable to obtain compensation for property confiscated by the new republic, they turned for help to the British authorities. On the whole, the rewards for loyalty were generous. Most of those who gathered along the Atlantic seaboard were granted land in New Brunswick or Nova Scotia. The Saint John River Valley, never really settled by the French, was a major area of occupation, and the City of Saint John, New Brunswick, prides itself on its Loyalist origin. In Nova Scotia most of the rich Annapolis Valley was already occupied by 'planter' families, but some of the Loyalists could afford to purchase respectable farms from the earlier settlers. Other families obtained grants in the southern part of the Valley, or along the south-west coast.

For those Loyalists who gathered along the St Lawrence River, there was still some room to the south-east, in what came to be called the Eastern Townships of Quebec. Elsewhere the fertile farm land was in the possession of French families that had held it for generations. To the west, however, along the north shore of Lake Ontario, and in the peninsula bounded by Lake Ontario, Lake Erie, and Lake Huron, there were thousands of acres of rich land, requiring only the woodsman's axe and the settler's plough to make them into farms. Here the settlement of Upper Canada began, the future Province of Ontario.

Next to their loyalty to the Crown, the most important thing that these exiles brought was their personal and inherited knowledge of frontier conditions and how to cope with them. They knew how to clear land, how to build houses, and what kind of crops to raise. The agricultural practices that they followed, wasteful to our modern ideas, were suited to frontier conditions. Excess produce had a ready market with the military establishments, who provided freedom from Indian depredations.

The first real settlement in Upper Canada was at Adolphus-town, 1784, but soldiers' families had settled at Niagara. The Loyalists spread east and west along 'The Front'. At the exit of Lake Ontario the village of Kingston grew up around a strategic fort and naval base. To the west the settlements of Napanee, Belleville, and Cobourg marked the mouths of important rivers. The excellent harbour of Toronto was bypassed, and the next important settlement was at the mouth of Niagara River, where the village of Newark was established across from Fort Niagara, now on American territory. This was the centre of settlement for Butler's Rangers and other groups that had been active on the British side during the hostilities. In the same class was a large band of Mohawk Iroquois, under the famous chief Joseph Brant (Tayandenāga). Their loyalty was rewarded by a grant of many acres along the Grand River, the first major stream west of Lake Ontario.

Among those who chose to remain under British rule were groups of Quakers and Mennonites from New York and Pennsylvania. Following their religious tenets they had remained aloof from the fighting, but they knew that British authority respected their claim to abjure killing, and they had no such assurance from the government of the new republic. These people came across the Niagara River and worked their way west to the Grand, but here they had to bypass the Mohawk grant and find free areas of settlement north-west of Lake Ontario.

All of the Loyalists who came between 1783 and 1789 were entitled to land grants, and in addition the government provided some equipment and basic rations. By an unhappy coincidence the year 1788, when the issue of rations terminated, was also a time of widespread crop failure and much resulting hardship. The tradition of the 'hungry year' remained with the Loyalists, and no doubt strengthened their natural impulses towards industry and the achievement of economic independence.

The new colony of Upper Canada was officially established in 1791, with the capital at Newark. The first Lieutenant-Governor was Colonel John Graves Simcoe, who had commanded the Queen's Rangers during the war. Although in office for only six years, Simcoe shaped the foundations of the future Province of Ontario. He encouraged settlement, built roads, and established a working relationship with the American authorities even while he distrusted them. In 1794, acting on the instructions of Lord Dorchester, the Governor-General, he moved the provincial

POST-LOYALIST IMMIGRATION

capital from Newark to Toronto, which he renamed York. Part of the reason for the move was the fine harbour at the mouth of the Don River, but also it put some 20 miles of water and 80 miles of land between the new capital and the American base at Fort Niagara.

POST-LOYALIST IMMIGRATION

Although the sponsored settlement of the Loyalists came to an official end in 1789, Upper Canada was still sparsely settled, so further immigration from the United States was encouraged. Large numbers of settlers took up land west of Niagara and north of 'The Front' on Lake Ontario. These newcomers had to take the oath of allegiance, but they were still looked upon with suspicion by the Loyalists, and their new allegiance was put to the test in 1812, when the United States declared war on Britain and prepared to invade Canada. Some of the 'Yankee' settlers followed their natural sympathies and supported the American forces, and in the end lost their newly-acquired land. Others remained loyal to their oath, but these events created a social barrier that took many years to remove.

After 1814, when peace was restored in Europe and North America, there was much unemployment in Britain, both agricultural and industrial. British North America seemed an ideal place in which to relocate the surplus population, and a government policy of sponsored emigration was begun in 1815 and continued until 1855. This was augmented by contributions from parishes and landowners, and by funds supplied by relatives already settled in America. In those days a westward Atlantic crossing under sail could take from 25 days to more than two months. Even in the best of ships there were many discomforts, but in the converted lumber vessels living conditions were incredibly bad. Crowded sleeping space, bad ventilation and sanitary arrangements, insufficient and inedible food, inadequate and fouled water supply, drunkenness and brutality among passengers or crew, all made the passage a ghastly experience. To these in the 1830s and 1840s was added the horror of contagious disease. Hundreds died on shipboard or in quarantine after landing, of cholera, ship's fever (typhus), diphtheria, and smallpox. These epidemics were aggravated not only by sordid living conditions on the ships, but also by the poor physical condition and ignorance of sanitation among many of the emigrants.

Nearly a million settlers came to British North America during the period of sponsored emigration. The Irish potato famine of 1845–46 added another wave of home-seekers. Dispossession of the small tenant-farmers (crofters) of the Scottish Highlands created distress that was partly relieved by privately sponsored emigration. The most notable of such sponsors was the Earl of Selkirk, who set up communities in Prince Edward Island as well as in Upper Canada. Colonel Thomas Talbot, who had been aide to Governor Simcoe, obtained a land grant from the colonial administration on the north shore of Lake Erie, and created the Talbot Settlement, which survived the War of 1812 and went on to become the prosperous farming region of St Thomas.

By far the most ambitious settlement project undertaken by private organizations was that of the Canada Company, which was established in 1826, with the famous novelist John Galt as Superintendent. A large area between the Grand River and Lake Huron was purchased from the Indians, and settlers were brought from Britain and allotted land under long-term payment contracts. So the fertile area known as the Huron Tract was settled, but the success of the Canada Company aroused the jealousy of influential people in Upper Canada, and Galt was forced to resign. From then on the fortunes of the Company declined, although the settlements themselves grew and prospered.

Meanwhile the strip of original settlement along 'The Front' of Lake Ontario had achieved an enviable prosperity. To the north of it was a region of forests, lakes, and rivers, picturesque but too broken by water and by rocky areas to be a great farming region. Nevertheless it was to this part of the colony that many individuals and families of the English middle class came to establish new homes. Some were retired army officers, others were sons of good families. Many, like the Strickland sisters, Mrs Moody and Mrs Traill, were skilled writers, and left vivid accounts of frontier life. Opportunities for sport and adventure were part of the attraction of this area, which centred around the communities of Peterborough and Lindsay, but the ready access by waterways was another reason for settlement here in the days before the coming of the railways.

THE RED RIVER SETTLEMENT

Settlement of western Canada owes its beginnings to the same Earl of Selkirk who established communities in Prince Edward Island and Upper Canada. Since the founding of the Hudson's Bay Company in 1670, the vast area between Hudson Bay and the Rocky Mountains, known as Rupert's Land, had been under the nominal jurisdiction of the company. Fur trade was its dominant objective, and agricultural settlement was one of the last things it desired. But the coming of trade rivals from Lower Canada, after the end of the French régime, forced the company to establish inland posts to meet the competition, and by the time that the two main companies—Hudson's Bay Company and North West Company—merged in 1821, so-called forts were in existence at many points along the Saskatchewan waterways. The most flourishing, and the western capital of the Hudson's Bay Company, was Fort Garry, at the junction of the Assiniboine and Red Rivers, a location that gave access to the north, west, and south.

Senior positions in the fur trading companies, those of 'factor' and 'bourgeois', were mostly held by Scottish or English persons, but the majority of the staff were French-Canadians from the St Lawrence Valley. Many of these married Indian women, and took up permanent residence adjacent to Fort Garry. They relied for sustenance largely on the game of the country supplemented by provisions from the company store, but they did plant gardens and raise vegetables. These feeble beginnings, plus the weather records of the company, showed that the Red River Valley was capable of supporting an agricultural community. Lord Selkirk proposed to establish such a community by bringing out dispossessed farmers from the Scottish Highlands. Theirs would be a wheat-growing economy, like that of Upper Canada. He sought a grant of land from the Hudson's Bay Company, and when this was refused, he obtained a controlling interest in the Company by the purchase of shares. In 1812 the first group of Scottish settlers came by ship to Norway House on Hudson Bay, and the following spring made their way by the laborious river route of the fur traders to the Fort Garry area. Most of them moved onto land along the Red River south of the Upper Fort, the site of present-day Winnipeg. Crop failures from drought or insect hordes, floods from the low-banked river, bitterly cold winters, and the hostility of the rival North West Company, almost destroyed the infant settlement. The armed intervention of Lord Selkirk in 1817 helped to stabilize the position of the settlers, and after his untimely death in 1820 the two companies merged peacefully. The Red River Settlement, augmented by modest additions of emigrants from Britain, became a prosperous if isolated adjunct to the Hudson's Bay Company, living in harmony with the original settlers, the Métis or people of mixed French and Indian origin.

THE PACIFIC COAST

Following the overland expeditions to the Pacific of Alexander Mackenzie (1793) and Simon Fraser (1808), the Hudson's Bay Company and the North West Company established trading posts on the coast. The principal one was Fort Vancouver, at the mouth of the Columbia River, at the site of the present City of Vancouver, Washington. Soon the support of these Pacific posts became based on the sea, for even the long voyage around Cape Horn was easier and more economical than the laborious canoe and pack-train route up the Churchill and Peace Rivers and down the Columbia Valley. For many years the southern part of this region, called Oregon Territory, was under a theoretical joint administration of Britain and the United States, but was actually administered and protected by the Hudson's Bay Company. The influx of settlers overland from the United States, and the acquisition of California from Mexico in 1848, led to the establishment of American sovereignty over Oregon. So the Hudson's Bay Company moved its operations north to the territory that had originally been explored by Mackenzie and Fraser, and which had become known as New Caledonia. Fort Langley had been established in 1827 on the Fraser River at the upper limit for sea-going vessels, and at the south-east tip of Vancouver Island Fort Victoria was located in 1842. From these centres, the Hudson's Bay Company, safe in its monopoly, carried on trade with the Indians, and preserved British control. The presiding genius was Chief Factor James Douglas, who ruled as head of the Company on the Pacific coast, and after 1850 as the Governor of the British Colony of Vancouver Island.

In spite of fertile soil and salubrious climate these early establishments in what was to be British Columbia were for many years simply trading posts. Victoria, with its fine harbour, also served as a naval base. Some 60 miles up the coast was the coal field of Nanaimo, a source of fuel for ships and houses. This simple economy was shattered in 1858, when gold was discovered in the gravel bars of the Fraser River. The miners who flooded in, mostly from California, followed the deposits upstream like hounds on a scent. Hope, Boston Bar, Yale, Lytton, and Lillooet were temporary halts as local deposits were worked out. Finally the gold-seekers emerged from the canyon onto the more open interior plateau of the Cariboo region. Here, in 1861, the richest finds of all were made in the valley of Williams Creek, at a spot that became known as Barkerville, after one of the more successful miners. This was about 460 miles by river and trail from Fort Langley.

This great influx of miners, mostly Americans, might have resulted in the annexation of New Caledonia to the United States, just as the rush of American settlers had led to the taking over of Oregon Territory. But Governor Douglas, although he had no legal authority on the mainland, demanded that the newcomers take out miners' licences, and so acknowledge British sovereignty. In return he guaranteed protection from the Indians, who had been provoked by the high-handed action of the miners. Most of them were used to the weak authority of the American frontier, but a detachment of Royal Engineers, and a fearless and ubiquitous magistrate, Matthew Begbie, enforced justice and maintained British rule.

As in most gold rushes, many came too late to have a share of the treasure. In 1862 a large party of young men from Canada made their way overland across the prairies and mountains, only to find all the gold-bearing areas already claimed. But many of them stayed to farm the fertile Fraser Valley below the canyon, or to exploit the rich timberland of the Cariboo.

The greatest need of the new El Dorado was a means of access. From Fort Langley to the mouth of the canyon at Fort Hope the Fraser River was navigable by small steamboats. Governor Douglas authorized the construction of a wagon road from Fort Hope through the canyon, under the direction of the Royal

3 Outline map of northern North America, showing (stipple pattern) the areas of the British Colonies in 1866, just prior to the establishment of the Dominion of Canada

Engineers, but with most of the work done by civilian contractors. It took four years to extend the road to Barkerville, but a life-line had been thrust into the British Columbia interior.

As a base of supplies for the construction of the road and the inland empire that was created, Fort Langley was on the wrong side of the river. A new settlement, farther downstream and on the north bank, was located and named New Westminster. Victoria, on Vancouver Island, remained the seat of government. In 1866 the Colony of Vancouver Island was finally united with the mainland as the new Colony of British Columbia.

2

The Farms

Throughout the colonial history of Canada the great majority of settlers came from the agricultural classes of their home lands: French peasants, American farmers, English farm labourers, Scottish crofters, Irish potato farmers. Except for the Loyalists, few of them had actually owned land, although some had been tenant farmers. It was the lure of land ownership that drew so many of these people to the new country, a status that was beyond their wildest aspirations in the old. Even when, in the nineteenth century, unemployed industrial workers, or even city slum dwellers, made up a significant portion of the emigrants, it was to the undeveloped areas that they came, seeking cheap land and the life of the independent farmer. At the other end of the scale, educated people of the middle class, or even the sons of landed gentry, had no other purpose in emigrating than to take up land. Often the lack of agricultural experience led to eventual failure by such people. Many returned home, but others stayed to become prominent in business or politics, fields for which their backgrounds had prepared them more adequately.

THE FRENCH SYSTEM
Under the French régime, land was apportioned by the seigniorial system. This was a feudal arrangement, with real ownership remaining with the king. The seigniors were people of better class: officers of the army, or the sons of noble or wealthy families. Even religious establishments held seigniories. All these seigniories were feudal fiefs, the holding of which carried various obligations to the crown, including the settling of farmers on the land. The settlers, called *censitaires*, were obliged to render annual tribute to the seignior, either in cash or in some portion of their harvest, or both. They were also required to help build roads, and to provide

military service in emergencies. Superficially the system seems little better than the near-serfdom under which the French peasants existed in the seventeenth century. Actually it was vastly more tolerable. The censitaire, if he cleared his land, planted and harvested his crops, and rendered his dues of rent and service, was in other respects an independent farmer. He scorned the term 'paysan', and insisted that he was an 'habitant', a title that his descendants still hold in honour. If conditions on his holdings became intolerable, he, or at least his sons, had the illegal but attractive alternative of taking to the woods, for a life not much different from that of the Indians, and making a free living as a trapper or a trader of furs.

A seigniory might be anything from 100 to 1,000 acres in area. It was divided on the basis of the old French system of land measurement, in which the unit was the *arpent*. As a measure of length the arpent consisted of 100 perches of 18 French feet. As an area, it was 100 perches square, which works out to about five-sixths of an English acre. The allotment to a censitaire might be something between 20 and 60 arpents. But the shape was unusual, being that of a long, narrow rectangle, with the front, two or three arpents wide, a part of the shore of a navigable stream or lake. Thus the plan of the whole seigniory would be that of a grid, with a shore line as its base, and a row of long, narrow lots about 300 feet wide running back into the hinterland for a mile or more. The reasons for this unique system of land divisions were cogent. For many years after the establishment of New France, roads were almost non-existent, with communication and transport being by water. Hence access to stream or lake was essential to each settler.

Another reason for this peculiar lay-out of farm boundaries was the need for mutual protection. In the days of the Iroquois raids the farm houses were close together, and the settlers could assemble quickly at a place capable of defence. Even in time of peace it was a good thing to have neighbours close at hand in case of fire, accident, or illness. This method of land allocation provided some of the advantages of village life while still permitting conventional farming.

The seigniorial system, logical as it was for people with a feudal background, was not without its troubles. Some seigniors took little interest in their holdings, living like absentee landlords. Others failed to settle adequate portions of their assigned territory. For these and other reasons the rights of seigniors could be, and were, revoked. The censitaire, apart from being tempted to take off for a life in the woods, might, through indolence or misfortune, fail to perform the required clearing or tilling, or to provide the full rent. Subdividing the lot was another action against which stiff penalties were provided. In spite of these, artisans and tradesmen would set up their establishments on frontage of an arpent or less. This natural tendency was eventually made legal by the creation of villages at strategic points.

In most areas the seigniories were originally forested almost to the water's edge. The first task of the settler was to remove the trees. With little more than hand tools it was a tedious and strenuous task, and the complete clearing of a farm might require many years. In practice it was usual to leave an uncleared area at the rear of the farm, as a source of firewood or of maple sugar, and a place where partridge or squirrel could be hunted.

BRITISH FREEHOLD SYSTEM

The seigniorial system was extended to parts of the Atlantic region during the French régime, notably the Annapolis Valley and the settlements along the Saint John River. When New France came completely under British rule in 1763, the system was allowed to continue, and in fact was not abolished until 1854. But all new settlement was on the basis of the British system of freehold. In this the occupant of the land obtained ownership by payment of a fee to the government or by completing certain improvements, such as the clearing and planting of a stipulated portion. Once the title was secured the land was real property, to be retained during the lifetime of the owner and passed on to his heirs, or to be sold on such terms as he might decide.

The basic British land unit, roughly analogous to the seigniory, was the township. It had been used in many parts of the American colonies under British rule, and was familiar to the Loyalists and other immigrants from the United States. In theory a township consisted of a rectangle of 36 square miles, but in practice varied widely in size and shape. In Nova Scotia the lands from which the Acadians had been expelled were resurveyed into townships. As new settlers came in, additional townships were established. The boundaries were often irregular because of shorelines and mountains. Curiously, the land within the township was often left unsurveyed, the division into farms being left to the agreement of the settlers. This is one of the reasons why farms in Nova Scotia often have irregular and seemingly capricious boundaries.

Another source of confusion is the usage in the older records of 'town' for township, giving the modern reader the impression of an urban, rather than a rural, community. In Upper Canada the townships were laid out in a more nearly rectangular outline. Starting with a base line, which might be along a shore, or just the boundary with an adjacent township, a series of transverse lines, between seven and ten in number, were surveyed at regular intervals. The spacing varied with different surveys between 3,300 and 4,323 feet. These were called concession lines. The strip of land between each pair of concession lines was divided transversely into lots, varying from 1,254 to 1,320 feet in width, and of length equal to the interval between the two concession lines. The rows of lots were called concessions, and the lots in each concession were numbered serially, usually from west to east. Lots could be designated by number and concession, but the townships were named. Most of the names chosen were patriotic or commemorative, but some were capricious. When a settler obtained ownership of a particular lot in a newly-opened township, he first located one end of a bordering concession line, and then followed the line as cut by the surveyors through the forest until he located the numbered corner post of his lot.

Many townships departed radically in size and layout from the typical arrangement described above. The concession lines might be any direction but east-west, and the number of concessions per township and lots per concession could differ. An individual lot might vary in size from 150 to 200 acres or more. With all its variants, however, it was a system that could be understood, and that could permit positive identification of a designated property and its boundaries.

ACQUIRING OWNERSHIP

There were many different ways in which the settler under the British régime could obtain title to land. First in time was the outright grant. The head of each Loyalist family received a clear title to 200 acres and those who had served as officers in British regiments during the American war were given larger allotments. Sons of Loyalists also had the privilege of obtaining land when they were ready to settle on it. Many of these 'United Empire Rights' were never taken up by the original recipient, and became subject to sale or exchange. In 1833, when government land was selling at an average of 10 shillings (50p) per acre, U.E. Rights could be bought at 5 shillings (25p). It is said that on occasions the right for a 200-acre lot might go for 6 pounds, or even a gallon of whiskey!

Early British settlement in Nova Scotia antedated the Loyalist period, but even then grants had been given to officers and men who had served in the army. Similar inducements were offered to families from the New England colonies. When the Loyalist rush came, much of the best land was already taken. Later settlement was mostly by purchase of government land, or by leasing under a colonization scheme.

In Upper Canada, when a new township was opened for settlement, would-be owners would apply for the lot of their choice. The first applicant could pay the nominal fee and take possession, but this was not an outright purchase. It was necessary to comply with certain obligations, such as clearing and tilling a portion of the lot, and erecting some sort of dwelling. Most settlers under this system 'proved' their title within a reasonable time, but there were others who purchased for speculation, and who acquired their title by having the work done, or claimed to be done, by others. Later, when surrounding lots had been improved and roads opened, such speculators might expect to sell at a handsome profit.

Speculation was a serious threat to the orderly development of townships. Another, more notorious source of delay and complaint were the 'clergy reserves'. These were lots, usually 49 per township, which were set aside to provide a source of revenue for religious establishments. At first this benefit was reserved for the Church of England, but even when it was extended to the Presbyterians and Methodists, it was still an unpopular system, and one of the complaints that led to the rebellion of 1837. Usually the clergy lots were rented, and the fee might be reasonable, but often they lay idle long after the rest of the township had become a developed farming community.

There were many organized settlement schemes under which an individual or a company purchased large tracts of uncleared land, which was then sold to settlers on some sort of time-payment plan. The famous Talbot Settlement was of this nature. Then there was the Canada Company, which organized the Huron Tract between the Grand River and Lake Huron. In the 1830s, Canada Company Land sold for between 10 and 20 shillings an acre, as compared to the government price of 8 shillings. But the Company provided various services, such as the building of roads and bridges, and the establishment of town sites. More attractive was their lease system, which allowed the settler to rent a lot at an annual rate of about $2\frac{1}{4}$ per cent of the nominal purchase price, with option of purchase at any time.

Some settlement schemes were organized by individuals or groups for benevolent reasons. Discharged soldiers, or unemployed industrial workers, were settled by grant or by payment of a nominal fee. The projects of the Earl of Selkirk in Prince Edward Island, Upper Canada, and the Red River Valley were of this sort. In far-off British Columbia, agricultural settlement occurred after the gold-mining influx of the 1850s. In most cases the land was obtained from the government by payment of a nominal fee.

One method of acquiring land was by 'squatting', that is, by just moving onto unsurveyed land, building a cabin, and clearing and cultivating an area. Such procedure avoided waiting for surveys and paying registration fees. Of course the occupancy was illegal, and the squatter could be evicted, but in most cases he was able to stay until regular settlement began, by which time he was probably able to pay the nominal price for crown land and enjoy the benefits of his improvements. Squatting was most likely to be practised by settlers from the United States, who knew how to establish and maintain themselves under almost complete isolation.

CLEARING

With the exception of the Red River prairies, the areas of early settlement from Nova Scotia to British Columbia were originally occupied by dense forests, a formidable obstacle for the would-be farmer. Stands of what in other circumstances and places would have been valuable timber were to the pioneer only a monstrous crop of weeds, to be destroyed in the quickest and easiest way possible.

There was no easy way, however, only man-power, assisted perhaps by a yoke of oxen. Only experience and ingenuity could make the task a little less herculean. The axe was the principal, almost the only, tool. The early axes brought from Europe were little more than enlarged hatchets. We see the style in the so-called tomahawks that were traded to the Indians for furs, and which served them as combined implement and weapon. The blade was fan-shaped, the edge much wider than the socket, and the handle was straight, with a circular cross-section. Such an axe was awkward to swing and difficult to control, but even in the early nineteenth century this version was still being supplied to settlers.

Meanwhile, however, the American axe had emerged from the frontier. It had a head in which the main part or poll was almost as wide as the blade, and projected like a hammer head to provide a means of driving stakes or wedges. The handle was oval in section, and had an S-curve, which provided a more natural path for the right hand as it slid along the handle during the stroke. The tip of the handle was expanded to give a firm grip for the left hand, which remained fixed as the axe was swung.

Even the best of axes can be a clumsy and dangerous tool in the hands of an inexperienced chopper. Many serious accidents were caused by misdirected or deflected strokes. But with an experienced woodsman the axe was a craftsman's tool. Each blow fell exactly where intended. The fall of the tree was controlled with precision by chopping a V-shaped notch on the side to which the tree should fall. When this cut reached about the centre of the trunk, another notch was chopped on the other side and a little above the first. Just before the second notch reached the first, the remnant of the trunk would give way, and the tree, slowly at first but with increasing velocity, would crash to the ground just where the woodsman intended it to fall. The use of cross-cut saws and wedges in the felling of trees seems to have come late to the Canadian woods.

Before the chopping began it was good practice to 'brush' the area to be cleared. This consisted of cutting and removing all the underbrush and small trees. The best instrument for such work was the bill-hook, a kind of axe with a long blade, curved down at the end to form a sort of hook. It was, in fact, a heavy version of the sickle. The object of brushing was to provide the tree chopper with room to swing his axe, and also to remove impediments to a clear fall of the trees. A good worker could brush an acre of forest in about 6 days. The brush was piled in heaps or rows, and then the trees were felled so that their upper parts landed on these piles. Usually the trunks were chopped or sawed into 10 or 15-foot lengths, and the sections hauled away by oxen to be used for building construction or split into rails for fences. Often, however, the trunks were burned along with the branches. They would seldom be consumed at the first burning, and would have to be repiled and fired, a dirty as well as an arduous task.

A very slow but easy way of clearing was to 'girdle' the larger trees, that is, cut away the bark in a band several inches wide completely around the trunk. With its supply of water and nutriment thus cut off, the tree would soon die, but it might stand

4 Axes: left to right, trade axe, American axe, English axe

5 Stump puller, Lanark, Ontario

as a dead trunk for many years before falling. Meanwhile, however, the absence of a leafy cover would permit the land around the dead trees to be cultivated after a fashion, but only a poor crop could be expected from this method of farming.

The ash that was left after burning the branches or trunks of hardwood trees such as maples, elms, and beeches, was an article of commerce in the early nineteenth century. It was the principal source of caustic potash, essential for the manufacture of soap. It is said that during the War of 1812 the American dealers on the south side of the St Lawrence River continued to purchase wood ash from the Canadian settlers on the north or supposedly hostile side. Many settlers preferred to leach the wood ash and prepare the potash themselves. This was done by piling alternate layers of ash and straw in a barrel or crib. Water poured over this would seep through and dissolve the potassium oxide, and the run-off would be caught in a pottery or iron vessel. The solution was usually evaporated in a large iron pot over an open fire, hence the residue was called 'potash'. Another name for it was 'black ash', in reference to its dark colour due to impurities. According to Samuel Strickland, 25 shillings per hundredweight was a typical price paid to the settler for black ash. For soap making it was redissolved, filtered, and evaporated again to produce 'pearl ash'. Wood ash or its derivatives were among the few 'crops' of early settlement that gave a ready cash return.

The rate at which land could be cleared varied greatly with the density of the forest, the size and kind of trees, and the skill of the axeman. Those who were real experts, such as the men who cleared for pay, might do an acre in 9 or 10 days. Payment for professional land clearing in the 1830s ranged from 12 to 20 dollars per acre.

Even after all the brush and trees had been cut and removed, the land remained dotted with stumps, some of them several feet in diameter. In the early stages of settlement the farmer might try to ignore them, ploughing and seeding around them and harvesting with sickle rather than with scythe. Sooner or later, however, the stumps had to go. Stump removal was made easier if the roots were uncovered and chopped through. The stump could then be pried up, using a pole for a lever, or pulled out by means of a chain and a yoke of oxen. Later a 'stumping machine' was used. It consisted of a very heavy wooden tripod, with a stout, vertical iron screw mounted at the apex. With the tripod set up over the stump, the lower end of the screw was attached to the wood by a chain and hooks. The screw was then turned, like a capstan, by means of a long pole inserted in its upper end. The leverage was so great that heavy stumps could be raised by man-power, although oxen might be used if available. In later years a black-powder charge was inserted under the stump, and if well placed, could on exploding shatter the stump and make it easy to remove.

Stumps were not the only impediment to land clearing. In areas where glacial clays and gravels underlay the soil, boulders of granite or gneiss might have to be removed. This was a strenuous task, usually done by digging around each boulder, pulling or prying it to the surface, and rolling it onto a low sled called a stone-boat. It could then be dragged off by a pair of oxen to a dumping place, perhaps the boundary of the field, where it would help to form a fence.

The open, fertile farm lands that one sees today in the Annapolis Valley of Nova Scotia, the Eastern Townships of Quebec, the gently rolling hills of south-western Ontario, or the rich bottom lands of the Fraser Valley in British Columbia, give little hint of the enormous amount and intensity of labour once expended to bring such land to a state where it could be cultivated and harvested.

BUILDING FENCES

Settlers fenced their lots at an early stage of farm development, partly to mark the boundaries, partly to keep out stray cattle, sheep, or pigs, but mainly because the clearing stage was the time when fence-building materials were most readily available. The necessity of fences in an area recently cleared seems small, but cattle strayed, and wandering cows could damage even the crudest planting. Sometimes the brush from the first stage of clearing was piled along the lot boundary, producing a large but not always effective barrier. An old-time magistrate's definition of a legal brush fence was 'Fifty feet wide and damn high'. More often, however, the fence was constructed after the chopping, using logs or poles that otherwise might have to be burned.

Probably the pole fence was the kind most frequently constructed at this stage. In this, the trunks of moderate-sized trees were used, cut to lengths of 12 to 15 feet. To start, a couple of poles would be laid along the lot boundary, with their adjacent ends overlapping a foot or more, one above the other. Two long stakes were driven into the ground on either side of the overlap, preventing the upper pole from falling off the lower. Then more poles were fitted between the stakes, first on one side and then on the other, 6 or more to each side. The fence builders would then move to the other end of one set of poles, drive in retaining stakes, and fit the ends of a third set of poles to alternate with the second set. So a series of fence bays would be constructed from one end of the lot to the other. If the fence ended free, instead of turning a corner, short pieces of pole would be fitted in between the pole ends of the last bay, to provide spacing. Spreading of retaining stakes by the weight of the poles could be prevented by tying the upper ends together with a loop of wire.

Log fences were like pole fences except that sections of large trees were used. Individual logs might be a foot or more in diameter and up to 60 feet in length. The greater size of logs made such construction much more laborious than that of pole fences, but only three or four such logs were needed to reach the desired height. Sometimes the logs were drilled near their ends and a single retaining stake driven through the holes.

Easiest to construct was the rail fence. Rails were made by splitting logs or poles longitudinally, using steel wedges and a large wooden mallet. Rails were about six inches in thickness and something like 12 feet long. There was much variation in the way rail fences were made. The usual method was similar to that for pole fences, but sometimes retaining stakes were driven at a slant, so as to cross at the top, and a holding rail laid in the crotch. The snake fence was a variant of the rail fence, particularly common in Upper Canada. In constructing a snake fence the rails of adjacent bays were overlapped at a wide angle, which prevented them from rolling off each other, even without retaining stakes. Such a fence was a zig-zag of bays, rather than a straight line, and so could not be set right along the boundary. Instead, it wove back and forth in a marginal strip of six to ten feet in width. This strip was not accessible for cultivation, but at least the inner embayments provided grass for pasture.

One might assume that the stump fence appeared very early in the improvement of the farm. Actually it could not be built until the stump-removing stage of clearing, usually three or four years after the chopping. This kind of fence was made by aligning the uprooted stumps along the lot boundary, the butt pointing inward, and the spreading whorl of roots in a vertical position. Packed close together in this fashion, a row of stumps made an intimidating as well as an effective barrier.

In areas where stone was common in the fields, it could be used to make fences, while clearing the land at the same time. Limestone slabs could be laid like crude masonry, but rounded boulders could only be piled. Mortar was seldom used; not only was it arduous work to set rocks, but a cemented wall would be more rigid and more likely to break with frost heave. If the available stone supply were inadequate to build the wall to the required height, a low fence of poles or rails could be set on top.

Unless a wooden fence were very well constructed, poles and stakes would rot or come loose in a few years. Some inquisitive cow would discover the weak spot, and would exploit the leverage potential of her horns and head. Cows that learned this trick would repeat it wherever possible, but could be frustrated by means of a cow poke, a crude collar of three sticks joined in a triangle, or a flexible stick bent in a U-shape and secured with a cross-piece. Pokes were made for calves, sheep, and even pigs, although it is difficult to see how one could be kept on a pig.

Good fences not only prevented wandering of cattle and damaging of crops, but also preserved good relationships between neighbours. Many legal actions were taken over the destruction caused by stray cattle. In such cases it was important to establish whether or not the intervening fence was reasonably adequate. To anticipate and forestall such unfortunate incidents, some

6 Snake fence, near Nobleton, Ontario

7 Stump fence, near Woodbridge

townships appointed official fence watchers, whose duties were to inspect the fence lines, decide whether or not the barriers were adequate, and to demand the repair of faulty structures.

In the 1860s, wire became available for fence construction. It was smooth wire, and not very effective by itself, as even the tightest of strands could be squeezed apart by a determined animal. However, it was useful to supplement and strengthen rail construction. The wire strands had to be stretched between posts by some kind of lever, and latterly a special tool was available for this purpose. Barbed wire, which makes a really effective fence, did not become available until the 1870s, and was used mainly in the eastern provinces as a deterrent strand along the top of wooden fences. On the western prairies it played a decisive part in the transition from ranching to farming.

3

The Crops

Very often the first crop was planted immediately after the land had been cleared of brush and trees but before the stumps had been pulled. If the burning had left accumulations of wood ashes, these had to be removed or scattered. The soil, shaded for centuries by foliage, had no layer of grassy sod, and was easy to work. Some settlers, in fact, just scattered seed on the newly-cleared ground, and dragged the area with tree branches to give a slight covering.

TILLING

Some cultivation of newly cleared land improved the chances of a good crop. Often the implement used was a hoe or mattock. Even with the soft forest soil such work was slow and exhausting. An easier method was to use a crude harrow, a triangle of wooden planks, through which a series of wooden or iron spikes projected downwards. But this simple device, drawn by a yoke of oxen over a field dotted with stumps, could be tiring to man and beasts. A simple type of plough popularly known as a hog plough, was sometimes used in fields with stumps. It consisted of a stout bent pole, fastened near mid-length by rope or chain to the ox yoke. In use, the sharpened end was pointed into the ground, and the other end was used as a handle. Pulled by oxen, this simple device could scratch a shallow furrow, like the rooting of a pig's snout. A slightly more sophisticated device was the so-called Loyalist plough, consisting of wooden beam, mould-board, and handle, but with an L-shaped piece of iron for a plough share.

After the stumps were removed, more efficient implements could be used. The plough of early French Canada was the continental model, with two wheels in front to keep it erect. It had a simple metal share, but no mould-board to turn the sod. The alignment of the furrow was controlled by means of two long

8 Primitive harrow, made from a forked log

9 Early plough with iron share and coulter and wooden mould-board

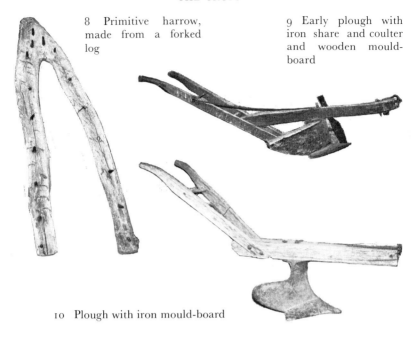

10 Plough with iron mould-board

handles projecting backwards. Although a great improvement over the hoe or mattock, this plough was never used extensively. It was expensive to build, and it broke down frequently and was difficult to repair. By the time of English settlement, a plough with a wooden mould-board was in wide use. This was in some respects simpler than the continental plough, for it had no wheels, or at most a single wheel in front to hold the plough in the furrow. Good ploughing with such an implement required skill, for the ploughman had not only to hold the plough in the right angle and direction, but also to direct the oxen by prod or voice. Ploughing with horses came later; in fields with rocks or roots, horses could get out of control if the plough were suddenly caught.

After ploughing, the field was usually harrowed, and perhaps compacted by dragging or rolling a large log over the surface. This would be the stage for spreading fertilizer, but on land that had been cleared only two or three years, it was not really needed. Later, when fertilizer would have been helpful, most farmers still neglected this important aid to good harvest. In French Canada the authorities railed against the habitants who would not use the abundant manure provided by their cattle. In fact, it was often dumped into a nearby lake or stream. Visitors to English Canada noted huge piles of accumulated manure that eventually forced the farmer to move his barn. One soil additive that was used was crushed lime or gypsum, which improved heavy, organic-rich soil.

SOWING

Of all the field crops planted by the Canadian farmer, wheat was always the most popular. This was true in French Canada and in the Atlantic colonies, as well as in Upper Canada. Wheat gave a relatively high yield, was not too difficult to plant and harvest, and when the kernels were ground into flour, produced the most nutritious and palatable bread. Surplus wheat could be disposed of by sale or barter.

Wheat was planted either in the autumn or the spring, the former being known as fall or winter wheat. Sowing of fall wheat was usually in September, or later if the autumn were mild. Sometimes the fall planting sprouted too soon, and was killed by an early frost. But if all went well it would have a start of a week or two over the spring planting in May or June. This was important, because an early autumn frost could destroy a late wheat crop by freezing the kernels before they were fully ripened and dried.

There were many other threats to a successful wheat crop. One of these was the Hessian fly, the larva of which attacked both roots and stems in the early stages of growth. The wire worm, the larva of the click-beetle, also attacked the roots of wheat and other field crops. In the early days of the Red River Settlement, entire crops were destroyed some years by hordes of locust-like grasshoppers. Perhaps the most insidious enemy was rust, a fungus infestation particularly prevalent in years of abundant rainfall. There seemed to be no defence against this blight until the introduction of Red Fife wheat in the 1840s, a strain from northern Europe that was naturally immune to the infection.

Oats, barley, and rye usually were grown as food for cattle, although in late colonial times much of the last two, along with wheat, went to the numerous distilleries to make whiskey. Flax was grown to provide linen fibres for weaving. It was a long-stem variety, unlike the short, heavily seeded kind now grown to produce linseed oil. All of these field crops were sown by hand, the sower scattering the seeds with a sweeping motion of the arm as he walked across the field. His supply of seed was carried in a sack slung around his waist. In the nineteenth century various semi-mechanical seeding devices were introduced. One of these was a narrow wooden trough about 12 feet long, with a perforated bottom. It was carried slung from the shoulders and held at right angles to the line of march. A board with slots in it was moved back and forth in the bottom of the trough. Seeds filling the trough were shaken out through the holes.

Horse-drawn seeders appeared in the 1840s. A row of blades cut narrow grooves in the soil, into which seeds were dropped from a long box. The seed drill was invented in the 1850s; in this the seeds were not just dropped into the furrows, but were inserted into the soil through flexible tubes with a cutting edge in front. Early models had a tendency to jam or break, but today the seed drill is still the usual device for planting field crops.

The word corn in North America means Indian corn or maize. First grown as a crop by the natives of Mexico, it had spread to what is now south-western Ontario by historic times. The settlers adopted and developed it, and used it as food for man and animals. It was planted by methods very different from those used for other field crops. Usually a shallow furrow was ploughed, and two or three corn kernels dropped into this about every two feet. With every fourth group of corn seeds a pumpkin seed might be added; pumpkins grew very well along with corn. Another way of planting corn was to form with a hoe a row of little mounds about three feet apart, and insert the seeds at the top of the mound. The drudgery associated with corn growing, as well as the risk of destruction by early frost, kept this crop from being extensively sown until the introduction of mechanical implements. One of the first corn-planters consisted of a wooden box to hold the seed, and a long flat blade, the end of which could be thrust into the ground. By means of a sliding release a few kernels could be ejected from the box and down the blade into the ground.

Purely as a forage crop, field peas were easier to grow than corn. Millet and buckwheat were also grown as cattle feed, as were turnips. The last-named were commonly used for sustenance in winter, and were kept in ventilated pits. Where hay was harvested for cattle feed, it was usually the wild, naturally seeded grass, especially the high, coarse growth of marshlands. Planting of hay crops came long after the land had been cleared and used for wheat or corn.

A common criticism of the settlers in French and English Canada was that they planted wheat year after year on the same land, a practice that rapidly depleted the soil of its nutriment. 'Wheat mining' has been common among Canadian farmers from the first settlements until long after the colonial period. Of course the temptation would be great in a pioneer community to repeat a crop that had a high yield and a ready sale. But many farmers did practise a crude kind of crop rotation, alternating oats or barley with wheat, and occasionally allowing the fields to stand idle for a year. This dormant land or 'summer-fallow' had to be cultivated enough to keep down weed growth. Sometimes it would be used to raise a crop of potatoes or turnips.

HARVESTING

Wheat ripens slowly. First the heads turn from green to pale yellow. Then the kernels solidify, through a 'milk' stage and a 'dough' stage to a hard, dry seed. Spring wheat was usually ready to cut in late August, while winter wheat would be ripe a week or two earlier. Excessively wet weather could delay the harvest or even ruin the crop. A hot, dry summer could ripen the heads prematurely, giving a low yield of grain. In years of good harvest, poor roads might prevent getting the wheat to market, and low prices might partly nullify the reward of a bountiful crop.

In French Canada, and in the early stages of the English colonies, the ripe wheat was cut with some sort of sickle. Sickles used in Lower and Upper Canada had stout blades, but those in the Atlantic colonies were more slender and delicately balanced. In using the sickle the reaper stooped, grasped a handful of stems below the heads, and cut the straw with a nearly horizontal slash of the blade. The severed heads of grain were dropped to the ground, where the gleaners would rake and gather them.

Perhaps because of small fields and large families, harvesting with the sickle persisted in French Canada long after the coming of the English. In most of the colonies, however, the scythe

11 Horse-drawn seeder

39

superseded the sickle as soon as the fields were free of stumps. The scythe blade is about four feet long, and only moderately curved. It is attached to a wooden shaft at about a right angle, and so can be swung in a horizontal plane without stooping. Two short handles project from the shaft at convenient angles for gripping, and the shaft itself has a slight S-curve to give better balance and easier swing. The blade had to be kept very sharp, and the harvester carried a blunt whet-stone in a wooden or leather holster on his belt, and frequently used it to hone the edge. Although cutting with the scythe was hard work, it was much faster than with the sickle.

Early in the nineteenth century a modification of the scythe was introduced; this was the cradle. A frame of slender, parallel rods of wood was attached to the shaft behind the blade, and parallel to it. As the edge cut the stems of the wheat, the heads with their straw fell back onto the cradle, and on the back stroke were deposited in a neat row behind the harvester. The term cradle was often used to designate the whole implement. A good man with a cradle, it was said, could keep ahead of two men gathering the cut crop.

Whatever the method of cutting, the operation was followed immediately by the gathering of the crop into sheaves. In this task the women of the family often participated. An armful of the stems was gathered, and an additional handful was twisted into a loose rope and wrapped around the middle of the bundle. A simple knot held the sheaf together. Treatment of the sheaves prior to threshing varied greatly. They might be set up in miniature stacks called 'stooks'; this was good practice if the grain were not yet absolutely ripe. Or they could be gathered in a wagon and piled in full-size stacks, the uppermost layer arranged like thatching to shed the rain. This was common practice in French Canada. Perhaps the usual practice in English Canada was to store the sheaves in the loft of the barn, a possibility in the early days when crops were small.

Mechanized harvesting appeared in the 1840s with the introduction of the mower. This was a horse-drawn device with a horizontal bar about six feet long, with widely spaced teeth. A blade with wide, flat teeth was made to move back and forth very quickly along the bar, actuated by one of the wheels of the machine. As the mower moved forward and the bar was pushed against the standing grain, the oscillating blade teeth cut the stems neatly and quickly, and the operation proceeded as fast

12 Horse-drawn mower, with sickle-bar raised

as the machine could be drawn by a team of horses. But the fallen heads still had to be gathered by hand. The next improvement was the addition of a platform behind the cutting mechanism (sickle-bar), onto which the wheat fell and was raked off into piles by a second man accompanying the mower. From this it was a step to the reaping machine, which had revolving blades to push the stems against the sickle-bar and onto the platform. The latter was provided, either with a mechanical rake or a belt-like sheet of canvas, which deposited the cut grain in heaps or rows along the edge of the swath. The self-binding harvester came at a much later date.

If threshing followed harvesting immediately, storage of the sheaves was no problem, but if they could be safely stacked or stored, it was convenient to postpone the final stage of the harvest until after the fall ploughing. Threshing in early colonial times was not much different from that operation as described in the Bible. A layer of sheaves was spread on the barn floor, around a post or barrel, and oxen or horses were made to tramp around this in a circle, while the farmer tossed or raked the wheat to ensure that it was uniformly trampled. This treatment broke the heads of the wheat, and the kernels, with or without their chaff coverings, would settle to the floor underneath the straw. After sufficient trampling, the straw was raked or forked aside, the grain swept into a pile, and the operation repeated with another layer of sheaves.

Threshing by trampling was easy, but the separated grain was often dirty and unfit for flour-making. A better, if more arduous method was by flailing. The flail was made of two wooden poles an inch or more in diameter, one piece about five feet long, the other about three. A hole was drilled through each pole near one end and a loop of leather thong was threaded through the holes and tied, so that the two poles were loosely attached, end to end. The operator held the long pole like an axe handle, and swung it from behind his shoulder forward and downward, so that the short pole hit the scattered bundles parallel to the floor. Repeated blows of this sort, perhaps administered by two or more flailers, would free the wheat kernels as effectively as the trampling of oxen, and without the risk of soiling.

Whatever method was used to separate the kernels from the straw, the former were accompanied at this stage by a large amount of chaff. This was removed by winnowing. Grain was shovelled into a large oval basket or a semi-circular wooden tray, and was shaken so that the kernels fell to the ground, while the lighter chaff was blown away by the breeze. But the wind bloweth where it listeth, and so the fanning mill was introduced. It was an old English invention, but did not appear in British North America until early in the nineteenth century. It was a large wooden box, in which a revolving reel-like fan produced a strong draught. Unsifted grain was shovelled into a hopper, from which it fell through the current of air. The chaff was blown out, while the kernels fell through a sieve into a bin at the bottom. Motive power might be from a water-wheel, but more often it was from a treadmill worked by a horse.

Complete mechanization of the harvest occurred in the 1830s with the introduction of the 'thrashing machine'. In this the opened bundles were fed onto a moving belt and passed under flails attached to a revolving drum. By the 1850s the thresher and fanner were combined, in one machine, in which the sheaves were beaten, the grain sifted, and the straw and chaff blown out, all in one operation. The grain emerged through a pipe, and was caught in burlap bags which were sewn tight as they were filled, while the straw fell into neat stacks, to serve as feed and bedding for cattle. This combined device required a two-horse treadmill, or a 'horse-power'. The latter was like an oversize capstan, with horses hitched to the ends of the arms. As they were driven around in a circle, they caused the central shaft to turn, and the motion was transmitted to the threshing machine by a slightly sunken shaft which the horses could step over.

13 Threshing wheat with the flail. Seeding tray, wooden straw fork, and another flail in the background

14 Fanning mill

15 Rotary horse power

GARDEN CROPS

Garden vegetables were grown in quantity in the more established settlements, but on frontier farms, time was not available for the intensive cultivation that they required. The habitants grew cabbages and turnips, as well as lesser amounts of onions, green beans, and carrots, but potatoes seem to have been absent from their gardens. In contrast, potatoes were the most commonly grown vegetable in the English-speaking colonies. They cannot be grown from seed, but must be planted in the form of 'seed potatoes', which are prepared by cutting the whole potato into a number of segments, each of which must include at least one 'eye'. Planting potatoes was much like planting corn. The potato pieces were either placed at intervals in a furrow, which was subsequently closed, or they were dropped in little depressions, which were then filled by hoeing up a mound or 'hill' of earth. After the delicate blue flowers of the potato plant had withered, the stems were pulled, and any potatoes that did not come up with the roots were dug up, preferably with a wooden fork.

Although turnips were grown mainly as a field crop for cattle feed, there were also garden varieties suitable for human consumption. They kept well in ventilated pits or 'root cellars'. Pumpkins, probably the most popular vegetable next to potatoes, were usually grown in the corn field, where they required little

43

attention. Other garden vegetables that were popular in the early nineteenth century were peas, carrots, sweet potatoes and cabbages. Tomatoes were also grown for food, contrary to the popular legend that our forefathers regarded them as poisonous. By the 1820s, some tobacco was being grown and cured for local consumption, but the days of large-scale tobacco farming in Canada were far in the future. A small part of the garden was usually set aside for herbs such as savoury, sage, dill, and mint, which provided flavouring for food and drink. 'Looking after the garden' was usually the task of the teenaged boys and girls. This involved keeping the potato hills in shape, pulling or hoeing out weeds, and guarding against the incursions of pigs and chickens. The appearance of the Colorado potato beetle in the 1860s meant another task for the young gardeners, picking off the grubs by hand. Later these destructive pests were killed by spraying the plants with a suspension of 'Paris green' (copper arsenite).

Fruits were cultivated from the time of earliest settlement. The domestic plum was introduced by the French colonists in the seventeenth century. Later, apple trees were planted, which eventually produced good crops, especially in the area south-east of Montreal. The French settlers of Nova Scotia (l'Acadie) found that the great valley along the Bay of Fundy side, sheltered by the wall of North Mountain, was an ideal area for orchards, and apple culture has continued to modern times as the dominant industry of the Annapolis Valley. Orchards were established by the Loyalists along the north shore of Lake Ontario, but the southern shore, between Niagara River and the head of the lake, proved to be the most favourable to fruit growing. Not only apples, but peaches, pears, cherries, and grapes were being grown here by the late eighteenth century. American immigrants were especially interested in fruit cultivation, and introduced improved methods of grafting and pruning. To get best results with apples, a hardy type of tree is planted, and when this reaches a moderate size, stems from a productive strain are grafted onto the trunk. By the 1860s, apples were being grown in Upper Canada from the St Lawrence Valley to the Detroit River, and more than 70 varieties were available, varying not only in colour and flavour, but also in ripening time and resistance to disease.

In the Fraser River Valley of British Columbia the early settlers found another excellent area for fruit growing, but it was many years before transportation was available to bring the abundant produce to a remunerative market.

4

Domestic Animals

Cattle were the most important domestic animals to the early settlers of Canada. Most of these were either draught oxen or dairy cows. The raising of cattle for meat was a relatively late development, although there were beef herds on the open land of the lower Thames Valley and the marshlands around Lake St Clair. These cattle were mainly of the old English breeds of Longhorn and Devonshire. As there was little market in Canada, they were driven to New York State for fattening and sale.

OXEN
Cattle used for draught purposes were mostly rather small. The so-called Canadian ox was a stocky, reddish animal like an undersize Devonshire, but almost any breed or mixture might be used. Under pioneer conditions, light, less expensive oxen were preferred, because they were easier to handle on rough ground, and because they did not involve too large an investment which might be lost through injury or straying. Oxen were used mainly to draw ploughs, but they were also essential in land clearing to drag away the logs or the stumps. Wagons and carts were commonly drawn by oxen. The harness for oxen was simple: a yoke of some sort, from which a chain extended back to the load. Yokes were of two kinds. In the Atlantic colonies they were constructed from a heavy piece of wood about six feet long, each end of which was shaped to fit the ox's head just in front of the horns, where it was held in place with straps. In the Canadas, the more usual arrangement was a piece of timber shaped like a rounded letter M to fit over the necks of the oxen in front of their shoulders. This timber was held in place by sticks of willow or birch, which were bent into a U-shape to enclose the ox's neck and inserted into the yoke on either side of the shoulders. The term 'yoke' was used not

45

16 Yoke of oxen

only for this device, but also to denote a working pair or team of oxen.

Unlike horses, oxen were not guided by reins but by means of a pole or prod. Well-trained oxen would also respond to word of command, a shout of 'gee' turning them to the right, and 'haw' to the left. The corresponding commands in French Canada were 'hue' and 'dia'. Oxen had to be trained from an early age, and small yokes were made and used for training the half-grown animals. If one ox of a pair were lost or killed, the other was usually unfit to work, because it would not function in unison with a new yoke-mate.

Oxen were slow and exasperating, but they were placid, which was their great advantage over horses. They provided a strong, steady pull, and were not easily frightened. If the plough that they were pulling became caught in a root or rock, they would simply stand and wait until it was freed. Horses, under similar circumstances, might become startled and unmanageable. In spite of the essential service rendered by oxen, it is sad to record that many farmers mistreated them, working them to exhaustion, feeding them poorly, and prodding or beating them in a cruel manner.

Most settlers kept a cow or two for milking, in response to the needs of a growing family. Like the oxen, these cows were anything but fancy in their breeding. They were small, usually mottled white and red, and provided with sharp horns, which they could use to protect themselves and their calves against wolves or dogs. They were probably of mixed origin from Devonshire and Ayrshire stock. Except in winter, when they were kept in the barn and fed hay or turnips, they got most of their food by grazing. This might have been in a pasture field, enclosed by a rail or stump fence, but more often it was in the woods, where they were allowed to roam. Each evening the cows had to be brought in for milking, and this was the task of the children. There are many pioneer tales, with or without happy endings, of children lost in the woods while hunting the elusive cows. The search was easier if a bell were attached by a strap to the neck of one of the cows. These bells were rectangular in shape, and were made by local blacksmiths. They produced a peculiar clanking sound, which was music to the weary youngster after a long trek through rough bush land.

HORSES

In spite of the more suitable nature of oxen as draught animals, most of the colonists preferred horses, perhaps because these animals were traditionally associated with sport and with the land-owning class. The French administration tried to discourage the use of horses in favour of oxen, but with incomplete success. The French horses were of the Norman type, small but stocky, and powerful for their size. The Loyalists, and settlers from England, brought a lighter type, with longer legs, probably related to the hackney breed. Very powerful draught horses, such as the Clydesdale and the Percheron, were not popular with Canadian farmers, for they were not suited to all of the many purposes for which a farm horse was required. Not only did it have to pull the plough and draw the wagon, but it might take the family to church on Sunday in buggy or sleigh, or be ridden, usually bareback, in search of errant cattle. The farm horse had personality, which was remembered in after years with affection and exasperation. Some of these light horses had good bursts of speed, and this led inevitably to comparisons, and to horse races. Such contests were informal, and perhaps had only two entries, but they could be community events and involve the exchange of money or possessions in won or lost bets.

An exception to the preference for medium-weight horses was found among the German-speaking immigrants from Pennsylvania, who came to Upper Canada late in the eighteenth century. The heavy freight wagons in which they brought their

17 Shoeing a horse at Black Creek Pioneer Village, Ontario

families and possessions were drawn by large, black horses, similar to the German coach horse. Along with the wagon that they pulled, these horses became known by the name of the town from which many of the settlers came, Conestoga. In time, however, the preference for the lighter, more general-purpose horse prevailed, and the Conestoga breed disappeared.

Horses used for ploughing and short-distance hauling could get along with unshod hoofs, but for travel on roads, especially those with corduroy or macadam surfaces, horses had to be shod. Horse-shoeing in Europe constituted a distinct craft, that of the farrier, but in North America it was usually done by the black-smith, the same man who repaired wagons and sharpened plough shares. At one time horse shoes were shaped by the smith from straight pieces of strap iron, but by the nineteenth century, blank shoes were available, which required only to have the caulks formed or attached, and the shape adjusted to the individual hoof.

SHEEP

Sheep were raised almost exclusively for wool, which with flax was the basis of the colonial textile industry. Sheep were unsuit-able for bush farms, as they easily became lost or injured, and were very vulnerable to the attacks of wolves or dogs, but in cleared areas they did well, and survived the Canadian winters with a minimum of shelter. Early flocks were of a nondescript type, brought from the United States, but later more specialized breeds, such as the Lincolnshire and Southdown, were imported from England. It was desirable to have a few sheep with black fleeces in the flock; a small amount of their wool mixed with the

48

white in spinning produced the homespun grey colour that did away with the need for dyeing.

PIGS

Pigs were kept by the colonists from the earliest years of settlement. Pork was always in great demand, as in the salted form it was one of the few meats that could be preserved under pioneer conditions. There was usually a good market for salt pork with the government, to be used as rations for the army and for subsidized settlers. So great was the demand at times that large quantities were imported from the United States. But as it was the custom in the midwestern United States ('Ohio') to let the pigs run wild and forage for themselves, the imported pork was of an inferior quality compared with the Canadian product. Pigs in Canada were usually confined, and fed waste products of the kitchen, such as potato peelings, stale bread, and sour milk, but in summer they also fed on leaves and roots. It is not easy to keep pigs enclosed, as they can dig under fences or pry poles apart with their wedge-like noses.

POULTRY

Poultry were important in various ways to the settler's economy. Chickens were raised mainly for their eggs, which not only augmented the family diet, but also provided a source of cash or credit for merchandise. The flocks of early days consisted of medium-size birds, rusty red and black in colour, not unlike the jungle fowl that was the parent of the domestic breeds. About the middle of the nineteenth century, more specialized breeds, such as the Cochin and the Leghorn were introduced to provide better meat or more eggs. Tending the chickens was the women's responsibility, and the daily gathering of the eggs was one of the children's routine chores. Geese were kept primarily for their meat. A by-product was their feathers, obtained by plucking the birds twice a year, an operation that does not seem to have hurt anything but the birds' dignity. Goose feathers had a ready sale, as they were used for stuffing pillows, quilts, and even mattresses. Ducks and turkeys were also raised for their meat, but they required more care than geese or chickens, and so were not popular with the settlers. All poultry were vulnerable to the raids of foxes, skunks, weasels, and hawks, and there was not much that the owner could do except to try to exterminate the marauders.

5

Buildings

In the Canadian colonies shelter was particularly essential, for the winters were long and cold, and even in the heat of summer there could be drenching showers or days of heavy rain. Many kinds of temporary shelters were used by the European settlers, but they seldom adopted the Indian wigwam, which was a frame of poles covered by sheets of birch bark. Instead, they built some sort of rectangular structure, the simplest being the lean-to. This was started by placing a pole horizontally between two trees, the ends resting on branches about six feet above the ground. Other poles were then placed with one end leaning on the horizontal pole, the other resting on the ground, to form a sloping frame. This was thatched with sheets of birch bark or the branches of spruce trees. The other side of the shelter remained open, with a fire immediately in front. Ordinarily a lean-to would be used for one or two nights during a trip, but it often had to serve as shelter for weeks while space was cleared in the forest and some kind of house constructed.

FRENCH HOUSES
Among the French settlers of Acadia and the St Lawrence Valley were men skilled in carpentry and building. The dwellings of New France never went through a stage corresponding to the shanty of English Canada. The nearest thing to log-cabin construction was that used in the walls of block-houses, with squared timbers to provide protection from bullets. In the early houses the walls were made with a series of upright timbers dovetailed into a horizontal timber or sill. This created a row of panels, which were filled in one of several ways. The filling might be field stone and mortar (*columbage*), fitted stone (*columbage pierroté*), or short, horizontal logs. In the last, the ends of the logs

were cut to a vertical wedge, which was fitted into a slot in the upright timber.

Stone construction was predominant in French Canada. A style developed which was characteristic of the St Lawrence region, and which became known as the Quebec cottage. It was rectangular, with the door centred on one side of the building. One of the rooms on the ground floor served as kitchen and summer living room. The other, usually closed in summer, was the living room in winter. Bedrooms and workrooms were in the attic, which was roomy, thanks to the steeply pitched roof. This roof projected as an exaggerated eave in front, supported by special braces. From this developed the bell roof, in which the extended eave is at a lower angle than the main slope. This would hold the snow on the roof in winter, and provide shelter from rain or sun in the summer. By adding upright supports for the extension, and a platform below, the veranda was created.

18   French-Canadian log shanty, showing panel construction, Wood Mountain, Saskatchewan

19 Farm house and barn, Aulnaies, Quebec

20 House with bell roof and veranda, Aulnaies, Quebec

ENGLISH HOUSES

The Loyalists brought a very different tradition in house construction. It is commonly assumed that this was the log cabin. But it had never been used much in New England, where frame and brick were the normal constructions. The log cabin is said to have been introduced into North America by the seventeenth-century Swedish colonists, who settled in what is now the State of Delaware. From them it spread to the Pennsylvania Germans and worked its way up the frontier to western New York and thence to Canada.

The crudest form of log cabin was the shanty. It was made with poles instead of logs, and there was only a slight effort to interlock the corners and fill the spaces. The door might be simply an opening over which a blanket was hung, and the fireplace a layer of stones on the floor with an opening in the roof above. The unfilled spaces between the wall poles took the place of windows for light and ventilation. This was the kind of dwelling usually provided in government-sponsored or privately supported settlement schemes. Adequate for one or two men while clearing their lot, it was intolerable for a family with mother and children. Yet such crude accommodation was often all that could be provided for several years after the settler moved onto his allotment.

Sooner or later, however, the settler got around to building a log cabin. In this the walls were made of logs thick enough to be fitted snugly at the corners by means of a system of joints. The logs were peeled, because bark held moisture which could cause rotting. With round logs the simplest corner joint was made by cutting a rounded notch on one side near each end. This notch was fitted over the curved surface of the log below. Sometimes the ends were notched both above and below. In either case the free end of the log beyond the notch projected on one or other side of the corner, creating the characteristic log-cabin appearance that is considered picturesque today, but which was just a nuisance to the pioneer.

Squared logs could be fitted together much more closely, requiring little or no filling. They also permitted the use of more elaborate systems of cornering. The simplest of these was the lap joint, in which the ends of the timbers were half cut away. This provided a space in which the half of the opposing timber could fit. Lap-jointed corners were easy to make, but provided little security against displacement.

Probably the commonest type of corner joint was the dovetail.

21 Log house and barn, near Stittsville, Ontario

22 Squaring logs for a cabin, Black Creek Pioneer Village, Ontario

In this the timber ends were cut in oblique notches, so that the end was nearly the original size, but sloped back along the log to a vertical cut. The notch also sloped from one side to the other. If the ends were properly shaped, they would fit snugly together to make a tight corner which could not be displaced in any direction. It also was self-draining because of the sloping faces of the notches. A less satisfactory system was that of wedges and notches. A wedge shaped on the top of one timber fitted into a notch cut in the under side of the next timber above.

Spaces ('chinks') between the successive logs, due to irregularities of shape, were filled with clay, or a mixture of clay and wood chips. With unsquared logs the gaps might be so large as to require the wedging of sticks or poles along the line of contact.

The door could be formed by leaving a gap in the lower tiers of logs on one side, or could be cut or sawed out afterwards. Windows, if any, were usually cut out of the completed wall. There were several ways of covering the roof. In one method, semi-circular troughs of bark or wood were used. After a ridge pole and a few rafters had been installed, a set of these troughs was laid side by side, sloping from ridge to eaves, with the hollow side upward. A second set of troughs was then placed, hollow side down, over the first, so the edges rested in the troughs. Rain or melting snow would run off the convex surfaces of the inverted troughs and down the slopes of the others.

Another roof covering was the shake. This was a crude shingle, a short, thin board, usually of cedar. Shakes were laid like shingles, each row alternating with, and overlapping, the row below. As the shakes had no taper, they gave the roof a peculiar bristling appearance. They were usually made by splitting a short piece of log along the grain, using a heavy knife called a frow, which was driven down the wood with a large wooden mallet.

Shingles were made from shake-like blanks by tapering the surface with a draw knife. This was usually done on a shingle bench. The operator sat at one end; facing him from the other end was a sloping board on which the shingle rested. It was held in place by a clamp, which was attached through an opening to a foot pedal below. The operator could hold the shingle firmly with the pressure of his foot, or release it readily when the tapering was completed.

The first floor in the cabin was often just the tramped earth. This was very unpleasant in cold or wet weather. To make a wooden floor, squared logs were set side by side, or crude boards were laid over a frame of timbers. The boards were formed by splitting logs with wedges and a mallet. In most areas of settlement it was a long time before saw-mills were close enough to provide sawn boards.

Next to shelter from rain, snow, and wind, the most important

23 Log house with second storey and shingle roof, Franktown, Ontario
24 Shingle bench and timber drill, Doon Pioneer Village

thing in the pioneer cabin was the warmth from a fire. Most cabin builders tried to incorporate a fireplace in the course of construction. Unfortunately, to do this required knowledge and skill which were not always available. Badly constructed fireplaces had poor draught, and allowed smoke to escape into a room. They might even be a fire hazard. A simple but dangerous form of construction was a wooden framework covered with clay. The usual material, however, was stone. If limestone slabs were available, they could be piled like bricks and cemented with clay. Rounded stones required much more clay to hold them together. When bricks became available, these were used to make solid and spacious fireplaces and safe chimneys. A well designed fireplace was six or more feet in width, with the opening three or four feet wide and at least three feet deep. Two iron rings were set in one of the side walls, to support the crane. There was usually a recessed oven in the front wall of the fireplace, with its own flue and perhaps an opening for ash disposal. Often it had a cast-iron door. Some fireplaces were made very large, like miniature rooms,

25 Wood and clay chimney, Ball's Falls, Ontario

26 Log cabin, with stone fireplace and chimney, Ball's Falls, Ontario

27 Log cabin with brick chimney, Franktown, Ontario

55

28 The Helmoken House, Victoria, British Columbia; early frame construction

with enough space on one side for a bench on which people could sit and warm themselves on coming in from the cold.

When sawn lumber became available, log-cabin building gave way to frame construction. Methods of framing were English in tradition, but were modified to meet North American conditions. Unlike the log cabin, which could be set directly on the ground, the frame house required some sort of foundation. This might be merely a narrow ditch outlining the ground floor of the house, and partly filled with stones or gravel to provide a solid base. On this the sills were laid, consisting of squared timbers running the full length and width of the house. The corners were formed by jointing, as with the log cabin.

The walls of the house were framed with vertical timbers, those at the corners being what architects call the principal posts. They were braced at the top by horizontal timbers called girders. A side or end of the house could be outlined with posts and girders and raised into position as a unit. Within the frame, additional uprights were introduced, spaced two or three feet apart. These were the studs. All the vertical elements were secured to sill and girder by mortice and tenon joints. In making this joint the end of the timber was trimmed to leave a square or rectangular peg, shaped to fit into a corresponding hole in the top of the sill or the bottom of the girder. For added security the joint was drilled, and a wooden peg called a draw pin was driven into the hole.

The ceiling, or the second floor, was supported by parallel timbers (joists) extending between opposite girders. The roof was formed by placing sloping timbers called rafters, which ran obliquely upward from opposite girders to meet at the ridge. They were notched into the girders, but connected at the peak by mortice and tenon joints. The ridge was supported at each end by a vertical timber from the middle of the end girder; this was called the kingpiece. Rafters might be braced by diagonal pieces from the joist. Each unit of rafter, joist, and brace was called a truss.

The walls were completed by some sort of sheathing over the studs. On the outside this was usually clapboard, that is, boards nailed horizontally, with the lower edge of one board overlapping the upper edge of the board below. Inner sheathing could be simple boards with a coating of plaster, or a framework of laths, spaced to provide a good grip for the plaster. Roofs were formed with boards or planks nailed on top of the rafters, and covered with shingles.

The three-way joint of girder, stud, and joist was a difficult one to make. It was avoided by 'balloon framing', in which the joists were nailed to the sides of the studs, and rested on sill or girder.

After the settler built his frame house, his original log cabin might be used as a barn or cattle shed. But it would be small for such purposes, so sooner or later a frame barn was built. Being larger, barns required more elaborate framing than houses. The foundation was typically a seven or eight foot wall of stone and mortar, which enclosed the ground floor of the barn and the stall area for the horses and cattle. The sill was laid on top of this wall, and timbers stretched from one side to the other to form the floor joists. Because of the large floor area, it was necessary to have a longitudinal beam down the middle, supported at the ends on the stone foundation and at intermediate points by pillars.

The framing of the barn above the first floor was more complicated than that of the house. The four principal posts were not sufficient to support the long girders, so additional posts were provided. At the ends of the barn there were no kingpieces, but one or more pairs of intermediate posts, which reached the roof at some point on the slope below the ridge. Additional posts and beams within the barn provided support for roof and loft.

Such a complex frame was beyond the power of one or two men to erect. The assistance needed was usually obtained by having a 'barn-raising bee', in which social pleasure was combined with constructive work. The farmer whose barn was being built had to provide all the materials: timbers, boards and nails, and plenty of food and whiskey for the workers. Preparation of the food was the responsibility of the farmer's wife, assisted perhaps by neighbours. On the appointed day the workers assembled, with their tools, and some of them with oxen or horses. One man, because of his knowledge and experience, was the framer, and under his direction the timbers were raised into position.

29 Pennsylvania-type barn, Black Creek Pioneer Village

30 Eight-sided barn, Downsview, Ontario

Entrance to the ground floor of the barn was through doorways left in the masonry wall. The second floor, which was mainly for storage of hay and grain, usually had its door on one side, which was reached by an earth ramp. In the Atlantic colonies, earth might be built up on both sides of the barn, with the entrance to the second floor at one end. In the style of barn brought to Upper Canada by the Pennsylvania Germans, the second floor on the side opposite its door extended out beyond its foundation for several feet, providing some outside shelter for animals.

Eight-sided barns were built in the Canadas (Quebec and Ontario), presumably based on the theory of an American, O. S. Fowler, that the octagonal form had many advantages over the rectangular in buildings. In the eight-sided barn the stalls on the ground floor are in a circle, and taper to the centre, where the mangers are installed. The stalls are reached from a corridor around the periphery. The second floor, as in rectangular barns, is for feed and grain, and is reached by an outside ramp.

NAILS

Although some sort of joint was generally used for connecting the heavier parts of building frames, nails were plentifully employed for floors, sheathing, and wallboards. In balloon framing, heavy spikes were used instead of joints. The making of iron nails goes back to Roman times. At the beginning of the colonial history of Canada, nails were made by hand from thin iron rods. These rods were cut from sheet iron by passing it through a set of square-cut wheels. The upper and lower wheels sheared against each other like rotary scissors. From the rod the blacksmith cut pieces of suitable length, and beat them to a tapering point at one end and more or less rounded head at the other. Hand-wrought nails can be recognized by their square cross-section, and a taper that is the same on all four sides.

A machine for cutting nails was invented in Massachusetts in 1810. It consisted of a heavy knife capable of slicing off narrow strips from the edge of a piece of iron, the width of which corresponded to the length of the nail. Each time the blade went up the clamp holding the iron would swing a little, first to one side, then to the other. As a result, the edge of the iron would be slightly oblique to the blade of the knife with each cut. Nails produced by this process have a taper on only two sides. The heads were formed by hand.

Wire nails, made by a machine that draws iron wire, appeared in the 1870s. They are distinguished by a circular cross-section, and a flat, machine-made head. The type of nail used is often helpful in working out the history of early buildings.

MASONRY AND BRICK

Stone construction for buildings in English Canada was mainly in areas where limestone was readily available, such as in the vicinity of Kingston, and the Niagara Peninsula. Limestone can be quarried and shaped into blocks, and laid like oversize bricks. Sandstone can be handled similarly. Many of the buildings in Bytown (the future Ottawa) were built of local sandstone. Where the more irregular field stones were used, much more mortar was required to fill the irregular spaces.

Although bricks for buildings were available from an early stage in the settlement of Canada, some houses were built from clay blocks which were simply dried in the sun. To provide strength and avoid cracking, straw was mixed with the clay. The clay was worked with water to a plastic consistency, usually by treading.

A somewhat harder type of clay block was made by baking it in an oven. Elaborate buildings, including one church, were constructed of this material. On the western plains, where timber for construction was far away, small buildings were made using blocks of sod cut from the prairie surface. These 'sod shanties' were crude, and did not stand up well, but they served until sawn boards became available.

True bricks are made by firing clay blocks at a temperature high enough to bring about chemical change. Old-time bricks varied widely in size and shape, but for more than a century the standard brick has measured 9 by $4\frac{1}{2}$ by 2 inches. Clay for brick-making has to be worked thoroughly. Until about the middle of the nineteenth century the working was done with shovels, or by squeezing between rollers. In old-time brick-making the worked clay was mixed with a proportion of sand. This was called tempering, and it made the bricks stronger and less likely to crack. The dough-like clay mixture was then pressed into frames, the inside dimensions of which were those of the brick. Sand was used to keep the clay from sticking. The loose bottom of the frame had a piece of wood projecting up to create a hollow in what would be the top of the brick. This helped to hold the mortar. After the frame was filled with clay a flat piece of wood was drawn across the top to make a smooth surface. The clay block was then turned out of the frame and stacked with others in the form of a kiln. This was a rectangular pile, with a hollow interior, in which a fire was set and allowed to burn for several days. After the bricks had cooled, the kiln was taken apart and the hard bricks stacked ready for use.

The familiar reddish colour of bricks is due to the oxidation of the iron in the clay during firing. To produce a cream-coloured brick a clay with low iron content was used. Dark grey bricks were made by firing at a higher temperature than in the normal operation.

The usual brick wall for a building was nine inches thick. If the bricks were laid parallel with the wall face, two tiers would be needed to provide the thickness. If laid transversely, only one brick was needed. Each layer of bricks was called a course; the parallel arrangement was a stretching course and the transverse a heading course. To obtain a solid wall it was necessary to have the junction between adjacent bricks of a course alternate with those of the courses above and below.

The cementing material between bricks and courses was

31 The Heck House at its original site near Maitland, Ontario; masonry construction

32 Lime Kiln, Ball's Falls, Ontario. The wooden superstructure is modern

mortar. This was a mixture of slaked lime (calcium hydroxide), sand, and water. The lime was made by piling crushed limestone in a ventilated pit, with alternating layers of firewood. The latter was ignited, and the high temperature of the fire converted the calcium carbonate into calcium oxide (quick lime). Lime kilns were common in Canada in the nineteenth century, as relatively pure limestone was available in many places. Before being mixed with sand to make mortar, the lime was 'slaked' by stirring with water in a trough. A boiling reaction occurred, producing calcium hydroxide (slaked lime). The setting of mortar was due to the reaction of the calcium hydroxide with the carbon dioxide of the air, producing calcium carbonate, and recreating, as it were, the original limestone. The sand in the mortar provided porosity, which allowed access of the air.

Some limestones used for making lime had clay impurities. Mortar made with lime from such a source would set to a kind of concrete. Such limestones were called water limes, and the product of their burning, hydraulic cement. From this it was just a step to Portland cement, which was first made by firing clay and chalk together. Later, ground limestone and shale were used. Mixed with water, Portland cement recrystallizes to a stone-like concrete. In practice the cement is mixed with a large proportion of sand or gravel. In colonial times, concrete was used mainly to form the foundations of buildings in place of stone or brick.

PAINT

Pioneer buildings were usually left unpainted. Even if paint were available, it was usually beyond the purchasing power of the settler. Also the time required to paint a building seemed better spent on more essential tasks. So the log cabin or the frame barn soon assumed the dull grey colour of weathered wood. Whitewash, a watery suspension of lime, might be applied instead of paint. It improved the appearance of the building, and helped to preserve the wood. It was also a mild disinfectant for the barn and sheds.

When linseed oil and turpentine became readily available, painting the farm buildings was more usual. Neat, well-painted buildings were particularly characteristic of the settlers of German origin. The cheapest pigment was the red oxide of iron, so red barns became common, adding a touch of colour to the rural landscape. Houses were usually painted with white lead (a mixture of lead oxide and lead carbonate), with trim of red or buff.

ROOT CELLARS

The root cellar was an important annexe to the kitchen. In it could be stored potatoes, turnips, and other vegetables. It might be a simple pit with an air vent, or a roofed-over excavation with steps leading down to a door. To be effective the root cellar had to be deep enough to keep out frost and sufficiently ventilated to prevent decomposition. Cases were recorded of persons being overcome by the fumes of decaying vegetables in root cellars that were too well sealed. In summer the root cellar provided a cool place for the storage of milk, butter, and eggs.

WELLS

A water supply for man and animals was a basic necessity. In the early stages of settlement it was usually possible to pick a lot near a lake, stream, or spring. As the back concessions were taken up, it became necessary to have wells. They might be made simply by enlarging an existing spring, but where there was no surface flow, the decision as to where the well should be located was difficult. Conveniently near to house and barn was about as good a basis for the choice as any, but many farmers tried to make sure that they would strike water before undertaking the laborious and sometimes dangerous task of digging for it. For this purpose the services of a water deviner or 'dowser' were often sought; there was usually someone in the community who claimed the special powers. Dowsing was widely accepted as a reliable way of locating the site for a good well, but as one sceptical observer noted, the occurrence of underground water was so general that the odds were greatly on the side of success.

Although crude methods of drilling wells were known from the early part of the nineteenth century, the farmyard wells of colonial times were dug by hand. This meant that one man had to pry loose the clay or sand and shovel it into a bucket, which was pulled to the surface and emptied by a helper, with or without the aid of a windlass. In most cases the hole had to be dug only ten or fifteen feet to reach ground water. Even such depths, however, could be dangerous for the digger, and lives were lost through collapse of the walls. This could be prevented by bracing the walls with poles or boards, but at the cost of additional labour and a longer time to complete the well.

After water had been reached and an adequate flow assured, the mouth of the well was lined with a box-like crib of poles or boards, usually with a cover. This kept debris out of the well, and prevented children and animals from falling in. The water was raised to the surface in a wooden bucket, which was like a miniature barrel but with straight, slightly tapering staves. A windlass, a small log supported on two uprights from the crib with a handle at one end, was usually installed. The bucket rope was wound around the log, so that the bucket could be raised or lowered by turning the crank.

Another device for raising the water bucket was the counterbalanced pole. A pole about 15 feet long was pivoted on a post beside the well, the part of the pole on the well side being longer than the part away from the well. The bucket rope was attached to the long end of the pole and a counterweight of rocks was tied or enclosed at the other. The empty bucket was lowered by pulling

33 The beginning of a well. Black Creek Pioneer Village, Ontario

34 Wooden pump, with iron handle and piston. Albion Hills, Ontario.

down the long arm, and when filled with water, was raised without much effort with the help of the counterweight. If the pole were pivoted horizontally as well as vertically, the full bucket could be swung to the side and detached, or emptied into a water trough. This method of raising the water would only work with very shallow wells.

Early water pumps were constructed almost entirely of wood. The pipe was made by boring out the centre of a log, and the shaft consisted of a long pole. Pistons were of various forms, the commonest being a wooden cylinder of a diameter to fit loosely within the pipe. The cylinder was open at the bottom and partly open at the sides. A wooden plug fitted loosely into the lower opening. When the piston was pushed down into the water by depressing the shaft, the plug would be forced up by water pressure, allowing the water to flow into the piston and out the sides. When the piston was raised, the plug would fall back, and the whole piston would lift the water up the pipe. This action, repeated rapidly, would eventually bring a column of water to the surface.

The uppermost section of the well pipe was usually squared, and provided with a wooden handle to raise and lower the shaft and a spout through which the water would emerge. Metal pumps were introduced about the middle of the nineteenth century. Because a much more tightly fitting piston could be used in a metal pipe, these pumps worked by suction. The short shaft had a piston with a leather diaphragm, which had to be wetted ('primed') by pouring a little water into the pump. Thus sealed, the piston, by its up and down motion, created sufficient vacuum in the pipe to lift the water to spout level. Such simple pumps were often set up in the kitchen with a pipe going down to a cistern in the cellar, which was filled with water from the well, or perhaps with rain water collected by means of eaves troughs.

6

Furniture

Very little furniture was brought to Canada by the pioneer immigrants. The exception was the chest, which functioned as a container for clothing and bedding en route, and later as a household receptacle and temporary table. Many of the early French settlers were skilled in some form of wood working; the authorities of New France recognized four different branches of the craft. So it was not long before the cottages of the habitants contained a simple but adequate set of furniture, and the house of the seignior held items of fine workmanship. The styles were based on those currently in vogue in the provinces of France, but modified to suit the local woods and to provide a more robust construction. So a tradition of good furniture grew up among the French Canadians that survived the French régime. Today the products of those skilled craftsmen are much in demand as 'antiques', and there has been a revival in Quebec of the production of hand-made furniture.

Among the early English-speaking settlers there were few who had any experience in furniture-making. The Loyalists were mostly farmers; those who came from the towns were merchants and local officials. Later settlement schemes, both governmental and private, tried to induce participation of persons qualified in various trades, but it was mainly local demand that led individuals to set up as furniture makers in the Atlantic colonies and in Upper Canada. The styles that they followed were those of England inherited through the American colonies.

The greatest departure by Canadian furniture makers from the European traditions was in the kind of woods used. Among the French craftsmen, pine was by far the most popular. It was easy to work, straight-grained with few knots, and readily obtainable. However, being a soft wood, it was easily marred.

Another wood commonly used was that of the butternut or white walnut tree. Birch was especially popular for chairs. Ash, elm, or maple woods were used more sparingly, often in combination with pine or butternut.

In English Canada, pine was used mainly for very utilitarian pieces; for stylish furniture the favourite was maple, in which peculiar grain patterns, called curly maple and birds-eye maple, were exploited. Walnut, oak, and elm were used more than in French Canada. Local furniture makers imitated American and English styles, and many pieces were imported from both sources. Mass production methods, developed in New England, were introduced into Nova Scotia and Canada West (Ontario). In making chairs, for instance, one workman would concentrate on producing legs, all to a standard design. Another would make seats, and another, spokes. The products of all these different specialists would finally be assembled into the complete chair.

The three basic pieces of furniture were the table, the chair, and the bed. Various container pieces, such as cupboards, buffets, and wardrobes, came later in priority, if not in time.

The long, narrow tables of peasant households in France were found in the Canadian colony only as refectory tables in monasteries and convents. The habitant preferred a short table, and particularly one in which a portion of the top could be folded down when not in use. These so-called gateleg and butterfly tables were well suited to the small rooms in the pioneer houses.

As the standard of living rose, a demand for attractive furniture grew with it, and fine tables with turned or carved legs were imported. Local furniture makers met this competition, and produced imitations of European styles such as Louis xv and Queen Anne. Such tables were provided with drawers, in which cutlery and linen were stored.

Few, if any, nails were used in early furniture. The term joiner implied a man who worked with joints rather than nails. The boards of table tops might be joined by tongue and groove, a flange from the edge of one board fitting into a groove on the edge of the other. Legs were secured by mortice and tenon joints, or by drilling a hole through both top and leg, and inserting a peg.

CHAIRS
The chairs made by early French Canadian craftsmen had solid

66

seats, sturdy square legs, and H-shaped stretchers to brace the legs below the seat. The backs consisted of two slightly tilted posts and a single slat at the top for a back rest. Such chairs were a crude adaptation of contemporary French style, but were strong and long-lasting. A lighter chair was made with a frame seat, which was filled in by weaving twisted rush stems. The back might be left open, as in the heavier model, but being a lighter chair, it could afford to have two or three additional slats joining the back posts. This gave the chair its English name of ladder-back.

The Windsor chair, an English invention of the early eighteenth century, was popular with the English-speaking settlers partly for traditional reasons, but it was such a good design that in later years it was adopted by French-Canadian craftsmen. The back of the Windsor chair varies in the frame; there may be two posts and a slat at the top, or a single piece bent into an inverted U-shape. The essential feature is the set of spokes that extend from the rear of the seat to the upper part of the frame, being inserted into holes at either end. There were other variations. The fan-back had radiating spokes, the arrow-back had spokes suggesting in shape the head of an arrow, and the bannister-back had turned spokes, split longitudinally to provide a flat surface on the front.

35 Ladder-back chair   36 Windsor loop-back chair   37 Windsor arrow-back chair

Wood-working lathes, powered by hand or by water-wheel, were introduced into the North American colonies in the eighteenth century. Used at first to produce simple legs and rungs, they were soon being employed to create elaborate turned patterns. These, combined with carved backs, went to make up the so-called fancy chair, which was prized as a piece of fine furniture. Many of these, however, were made in factories using mass-production methods.

A set of dining-room chairs usually included one arm chair along with the ordinary side chairs. This was commonly a Windsor, either with separate pieces for arms, or with the curved back frame extending forward on each side. The rocking chair is claimed as an American invention, although it seems to have been used in some parts of continental Europe. Certainly it was popular in the American colonies and was brought to Canada by the Loyalists, from whom it spread to the French Canadians. In time it became an almost universal part of the household furniture, being especially used by older people or by mothers holding babies. Early rocking chairs were ordinary chairs with bow-shaped rockers attached to the legs. A special American development was the Boston rocker, typical examples of which were made in Canada. It has a slightly hollowed Windsor-style back, and a seat that is convex in front, concave behind.

Benches were used in colonial houses in place of chairs. A bench is just an extended stool or chair, designed to seat two or more people. A common type of bench in Canada had a Windsor back, with arms at the ends. With the addition of upholstery, the bench evolved into the sofa or settee, various forms of which were popular in late colonial times.

Early Canadian chairs were painted, rather than varnished, common colours being green and light brown. The backs were often decorated with stencil designs of flowers or scrolls. Slats were cut or perforated in ornamental shapes, and carvings were added to the top piece. In contrast to the solid or woven seats of ordinary chairs, the fine pieces of the late eighteenth and the nineteenth century had upholstered seats, covered with carpet material, horsehair fabric, or even silk tapestry.

BEDS

Early Canadian beds were little more than a rectangular frame with four legs, with the inner space filled in with boards or slats. To provide some resilience the rope bed was developed. A coarse net of rope formed the sleeping surface, but it would eventually sag. So one end was wound over a cylindrical roller, which could be turned to take up the slack, then locked in position.

In early colonial times the fireplace was the only means of heating the house, and the problem of keeping warm while sleeping was a serious one. The French settlers tried to meet it by the use of an enclosed bed (*cabane*), which was really a large cupboard. This kept out draughts and provided some privacy, but it also must have produced a state of near suffocation. In the four-poster the corner posts supported a frame high above the bed. This frame had a woollen or linen sheet on top and curtains on the sides. Drawing the curtains kept out draughts and provided privacy without completely cutting off the air supply. The tall bed posts were usually ornamented with turning or spiral carving.

The introduction of stoves for household heating in the late eighteenth century made the enclosed bed less essential, although it was retained for its privacy or elegance. Even in open beds, however, the corner posts were ornamented with elaborately turned designs suggesting vases, spools, or buttons, and distinct finials. There was a low head board, and probably a footboard, or the latter might be represented by a stretcher bar.

In the early nineteenth century the so-called sleigh bed achieved some popularity. In it the end boards were curved in an S-shape, in below and out above. This suggested the sweeping lines of the cariole or cutter.

The settler's mattress was called a tick, and was a wide, flat sack filled with straw. When the bed was made each morning the tick was shaken to separate the packed filling. A more comfortable foundation was the feather tick, filled with chicken feathers or goose down. It was commonly used over a straw tick, and persisted in rural Canadian homes until well into the twentieth century. Not only was the feather tick soft, but it provided additional insulation as the sleeper sank into it. Each morning it was fluffed up again by skilful manipulation.

CUPBOARDS

Chairs, tables, and beds are for man himself, but chests and cupboards are for his possessions. The cupboard was basically a chest with doors rather than a lid. Its simplest form was the buffet, usually with two doors, and with a flat top about the right height to serve as a table. Superimposing a set of shelves at the rear of the top created the dresser, which in spite of its name was part of the kitchen furniture. On the shelves the dishes were set out for easy reach, and there was still enough space on the buffet top for working. Enclosing the shelves with doors, usually with glass panes, changed the dresser into a cabinet. This was suitable for the

38 Reconstructed kitchen of about 1863, showing the mantel clock and dresser with ironstone dishes

39 Pine corner cupboard

40 French Canadian pine armoire

better china and glass pieces of the household. A popular form, especially in French Canada, was the corner cupboard, for it was a space saver.

In the bedroom the buffet-like cupboard served as a receptacle for clothes and bedding. By increasing the height, and using either four doors or two tall doors, the wardrobe was produced, in which clothing was hung. Another variation of the buffet was made by adding drawers. From this came the all-drawer container, the bureau or commode. A tall commode with numerous drawers was called a highboy.

All these variants of the cupboard were made and used in both French and English Canada, but the French craftsmen were particularly noted for their fine versions of the wardrobe or *armoire*. The doors of these provided a wide surface for elaborate ornamentation. This was divided into four or more panels, and within these various designs were carved, most often the traditional diamond shape. Other motifs used were intersecting diagonals, elaborate spirals, scallop shells, and in later examples, representations of leaves, stems, and fruits. The French-Canadian

70

pine armoire with carved doors is today a prized antique, much sought by museums and collectors. Towards the middle of the nineteenth century another piece was added to bedroom furniture. This was the washstand. It was a small cupboard, with one or two doors, which might house a large crockery wash basin and a water pitcher. Other accessories might be a soap dish and a smaller pitcher for hot shaving water. Some versions had rungs along the sides to serve as towel racks. The washstand with its accessories was a step towards a more gracious and comfortable way of life, with its provision of privacy and the possibility of warm water. At first it was mainly used in hotels, but eventually it became a part of every well-appointed bedroom.

Few of the early settlers could afford a clock, or even felt the need for one. Only government officials and busy merchants had much need to count the hours. However, a fine clock was a status symbol. In French Canada the mechanisms at first were imported, and fitted into cases made by Canadian cabinet makers. About the middle of the eighteenth century, clockmakers in Trois Rivières and Montreal began producing the whole timepiece. Under the British régime, clockmakers came to Canada from New England. The most famous of these were the Twiss brothers from Connecticut. Many eighteenth-century Canadian clocks had gear wheels made of cherry wood instead of metal.

All the eighteenth-century clocks had a descending weight to provide the drive for the mechanism, and a swinging pendulum to control the rate of movement. Called tall-case clocks, they were narrow and high to accommodate the long pendulum and the weight. Often there was a set of chimes to mark the hours, and the mechanism for this had its own descending weight. The clock was 'wound' simply by raising the weight to the top before it had completed its descent. We know these timepieces as grandfather clocks, but this name came from a popular song of 1876.

Early in the nineteenth century, clocks with brass mechanisms became available. They were driven by a coiled spring, a method that had been known for centuries, but New England clockmakers learned how to adapt this to a clock that could be made cheaply and by piece-work methods. Soon clocks from Connecticut and Massachusetts were invading the markets of the world, including those of British North America. Judge Thomas Haliburton of

Nova Scotia, the first North American humourist, chose a Yankee clock peddlar, 'Sam Slick of Slickville', as his fictional commentator on colonial people and manners. These new clocks were low and wide, and not very deep from front to back. The front was a glass door, clear above to show the square dial, painted or silvered below. When opened, it provided access to the holes in which the winding key was inserted, and to the short pendulum. Often there was a large label pasted on the inside of the back, with the maker's name and address and the instructions for operating. Most of such clocks that came to the British colonies were made by Seth Thomas of Connecticut, and his label often included the name of the merchant in Canada West for whom the shipment had been made. With their moderate height and shallow depth, these clocks were suitable for a shelf or a mantel top, and they became known as mantel clocks. Their price was low enough to suit the purse of Canadian townsmen and the more prosperous farmers, and their accuracy adequate for the needs of the period. But the tall-case clock continued for many years to be the choice of those who could afford elegance as well as utility.

7

Heat and Light

Fire, says the old proverb, is a good servant and a bad master. To
the pioneer Canadian colonist it was an indispensable partner.
It helped him clear his land, it cooked his food and illuminated his
cabin, but most of all it was his defence against the Canadian
winter. Without the fireplace and the stove, European man could
have had no permanent settlements in the northern parts of
North America.

FIRE-MAKING
European man, until the early nineteenth century, almost always
made fire by striking sparks from iron with a piece of some hard
rock such as flint. He brought this technique to North America
and retained it in preference to the friction method that he saw
practised by the native people. In fact, the latter adopted flint
and steel and abandoned their own method.

Ingenious devices appeared from time to time in an effort to
make fire-lighting with flint and steel easier and quicker, but in the
settler's home the method and equipment were traditional. The
'steel' or 'strike-a-light' was a short bar of iron, with a handle
attached at one or both ends. The flint was usually a discarded
gun flint, a rectangular flake about an inch long and three-
quarters of an inch wide. The third essential was tinder. Usually
this was made by scorching scraps of linen. All this equipment
was housed in a tinder box, a low, rounded can with a lid, on
which there might be a socket for a candle.

Sparks were produced by striking vigorously downward with
iron against flint or flint against iron. The red-hot particles of
iron falling on the tinder would, with luck, start a tiny ember.
Careful blowing caused the glow to spread, and if the tinder were
well charred and dry, produced a flame that could be transferred

73

41 Flint-and-steel outfit. Rear row: tinderbox lid with candle, 'flint' chips, tinderbox. Middle row: steel or strike-a-light tinder, quenching disc. Front row: sulphur-tipped splints

to a candle or a sliver of wood. The step from glowing to blazing tinder was the difficult one, especially in damp or cold weather, and to make it easier a sulphur splint was commonly used. This was a sliver of pine wood about six inches long, the tips of which had been dipped in molten sulphur. The sulphur-coated head would take fire readily when held against the glowing tinder.

Chemical matches for fire making were invented in France in 1805, and soon appeared in North America. To light them it was necessary to dip the match head into a bottle containing sulphuric acid. This complicated technique did not completely supersede flint and steel, which became obsolete only after the introduction of the friction match in 1826.

During the flint-and-steel period, when fire was so difficult to create, an effort was made to preserve live coals in the fireplace overnight. This was done by 'banking the fire', that is, pushing the embers together against a back log and covering them with dead ashes. If all went well, there would still be glowing bits in the heap by morning, from which a new blaze could be kindled. Too often, however, there was just a mound of cold ashes, and then the tiresome task of striking fire had to be repeated. Rather than do this, one of the family might go to the nearest neighbour for a few glowing embers, which were carried back on a shovel or in a lidded pot.

For the early stage of the fire, kindling was made by whittling strips of wood from a stick of pine or poplar. The firewood was prepared by sawing logs into lengths that would fit the fireplace, then splitting the sections with an axe. Almost any dry wood was suitable, but pine was easiest to ignite and did not give off sparks. Hardwoods burned less vigorously but lasted longer. 'Getting in' the winter supply of firewood was a regular autumn task on a Canadian farm, and a large, well-stacked pile of cut and split logs was a sign of industry and a promise of comfort.

STOVES

The fireplace seemed to satisfy housewives as a means of cooking until well into the nineteenth century. As a source of domestic warmth it evidently left much to be desired. In most homes there was only one fireplace, in the kitchen. At a slightly more prosperous level there might be a second in the living room, purely for heating purposes. Few could afford one in the bedroom. Even at best the fireplace was an inefficient way of keeping warm. It was a standing joke that the person who sought its comfort was roasted on one side and frozen on the other. So it is not surprising that stoves were introduced for heating long before they were adopted for cooking.

Stoves were brought to Canada as early as 1668, but they were rare and expensive. It was not until 1744 that stoves were manufactured in the colony, at the St Maurice forge near Trois Rivières. These stoves were simple iron boxes, made of heavy cast-iron plates bolted together. The thick iron, once heated, was very effective in radiating warmth. It was now possible to have a source of heat in more than one room. Sometimes an opening was made in the partition between rooms, and the stove set up in this gap, so that its heat was shared on both sides. The stove pipe, too, gave off heat, and this could be used by running the pipe through more than one room before inserting it in the chimney.

Early in the nineteenth century the simple box stove was elaborated by adding one or two more boxes on top, making the double-decker and the triple-decker. The extra chambers provided more heat radiation, and served as warming ovens for food. Another modification appeared in the 1840s. In this the fire box had an exit for smoke at each end. An arch-shaped pipe was attached at the ends to these openings, and the two streams of smoke passed up the arch to the top and entered the stove-pipe through an opening in the rear. From a simple square pipe the arch soon developed into an elaborate ornament, with cast-iron scrolls and finials. This not only made the stove more suited to the décor of a Victorian parlour, but also increased the surface for heat radiation. Some models even had an urn-like container within the arch, which could be filled with water to provide humidity.

Usually when the stove arrived the fireplace was sealed off with a brick partition. Some stoves, however, were made to be inserted into the fireplace. The best-known of these was the Franklin stove, an invention of the American statesman and

75

42 Triple-decker box stove

43 Parlour stove, with arch-shaped flues

scientist, Benjamin Franklin. It had a fire-box in the lower part, and an ingenious arrangement of flue and air ducts so that the heat was provided by both the fire and the smoke through a draught of air that circulated through the stove and out into the room. In addition to its greater efficiency, the Franklin stove was much safer and cleaner than the open fireplace.

About the middle of the nineteenth century a new kind of heating stove appeared, inelegantly known as the pot-belly stove. It was barrel-shaped, with a flat top on which a pot or kettle could be heated. A door in the front, with mica windows, permitted observation of the fire and the addition of fuel as needed. In spite of their name, these stoves were often handsome, with iron ornamentation or brass decoration.

In spite of the introduction of heating stoves for parlour and bedroom, the kitchen stove, like the kitchen fireplace, was still the domestic shrine, the focus of family life, and the source of physical comfort. In most rural homes, at least, the kitchen was the real 'living room' for all but the most formal of social occasions.

CANDLES

For most household activities after dark the light from the fireplace was sufficient. But in the more sophisticated homes, some form of steady, portable lighting was needed for reading, sewing, or just to grace a dinner table. Until well into the nineteenth century the almost universal source of domestic lighting was the candle.

Prior to the nineteenth century only two substances were available as the material for candles. These were tallow and beeswax. The latter was too expensive, or too difficult to obtain, to be used for domestic lighting, and was reserved for ceremonial candles in churches. Tallow, however, was available to almost any farmer. It was made by heating, straining, and resolidifying the solid fat of mutton or beef.

The other component of a candle was the wick. In making candles at home, twisted cotton string was used. There were two techniques for candle making: dipping and moulding. Dipping was the simpler but the more tedious. Moulding was quicker but required special equipment. In both methods the tallow was melted over a moderate fire, with a little water in the bottom of the pot to prevent burning. In dipping, the wicks were simply lowered into the melted tallow, lifted out, and hung while the tallow coating solidified. This operation, repeated many times, built up a column of tallow around the wick that was thick enough to stand by itself and provide the fuel for the candle flame. To increase the efficiency of the operation, five or six wicks were hung from a stick, so that they could be dipped simultaneously. While the tallow was cooling between dips the stick was supported between the back of two chairs, or between two poles stretched between two chair backs. Rotary devices were used. The stick with its freshly dipped wicks was hung from a spoke; other sticks with wicks were attached to other spokes. By the time any particular stick came around again its wicks were ready for another dipping. Among the French Canadians the solidifying of the tallow was speeded up by dipping the impregnated wicks into cold water, but this was likely to produce a crooked candle.

Moulds for candle-making were sheet-metal tubes, about three-quarters of an inch in diameter and 10 to 12 inches long. The upper end was open and the lower end was tapered to a small hole. Single-tube moulds were used, but more often the tubes were set in a frame, with four or more tubes to a set. First, the wicks had to be threaded in the moulds. The string was passed through the small hole at the lower end of the tube and knotted outside. At the upper end it was pulled tight and tied with a slip knot to a small stick laid across the opening. Usually a row of wicks was tied to the same stick. When the wicks were all tightened and centred, the mould was ready for the tallow. This was poured into the open ends of the tubes. It shrank on cooling, so that a second, or even a third pouring was necessary. After the tallow was cool and solid, the mould was dipped momentarily into hot water, which freed the candles from the walls of the mould tubes and allowed them to be drawn out by the wick ends.

Once a mould had been acquired, the making of candles by moulding was more convenient than by dipping. One important advantage was that it was just as easy to make a few candles as to make a large number, whereas dipping was only efficient when enough tallow was available to fill a deep pot. The candle mould was an almost universal household utensil in colonial Canada.

Tallow was far from ideal as a candle material. In warm weather it became soft and liable to bend. Commercial candle-makers added beeswax and alum to the tallow, and sold the product as 'adamantine' candles; they were harder but more expensive. Tallow candles were very susceptible to 'guttering', that is, melting unevenly, so that unburned liquid tallow leaked down the sides. A piece of charred wick, falling on the rim of the candle, would accelerate this wastage. The wick needed frequent trimming, which was done with a scissors-like instrument called a snuffer. The use of braided wicks helped to prevent particles of carbon or 'snuff' from falling. Another problem with tallow candles was that they were liable to be eaten by mice or rats, and had to be stored in a closed receptacle called a candle safe.

The first major advance of centuries in the art of candlemaking occurred about 1800 with the introduction of spermaceti as candle

44   Six-tube   candle
mould, Ontario

45 Candle safe, Quebec City

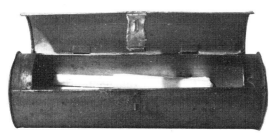

wax. Spermaceti is a hard white substance derived from the oil in the head of the sperm whale. Candles made from this material did not collapse in warm weather, and burned with a clear flame without guttering. But they had to be imported from Massachusetts, and were too expensive for most Canadian households. Another kind of 'store-bought' candle appeared in 1831; it was made of stearine. This is a chemically refined product of animal or vegetable fat, and candles made from it had the advantages of spermaceti candles without being as expensive. Most stearine candles came from England, where they were manufactured by machinery. But neither stearine nor spermaceti candles really superseded the tallow article, which could be made in the farm kitchen.

The refining of petroleum to produce lamp fuel began in 1860, and a by-product, paraffin wax, became available for candle making. This quickly displaced other candle materials, and has remained in use as the universal candle wax ever since. The dominance of the candle as a means of lighting was ended by the introduction of another economical and more efficient lighting device, the paraffin or kerosene lamp.

Almost any kind of tubular receptacle would do as a candle holder. The usual form had the tube supported on a saucer-shaped base. Inside the tube was a piston, which could be raised or lowered by means of a handle through a slit. In this way the candle was supported except for a short portion at the burning end, and could be moved up progressively as the tallow was consumed. Elaborate brass and silver 'candlesticks', and multiple candle holders such as candelabra and girandoles, were used in the more affluent households, but were more for ornament than utility.

Candles were also used in lanterns for lighting outside the house. A common type consisted of a large sheet-metal can, with a door and a conical lid. Light from the candle inside came through numerous perforations in the metal, and was rather feeble, but such a lantern was relatively safe to use in the barn, with its hay and other combustibles. A more efficient lantern was made of rectangular wooden frames put together to form an open box, the sides of which were filled in with small panes of glass. To permit access, one side might be hinged, or one of the panes might be set in slots, and was capable of being raised.

LAMPS
The lamp is an older means of lighting than the candle, going back

to prehistoric times. It differs from the candle in that the fuel is liquid, and has to be held in some sort of container. The simplest is the pan lamp, which was used in several forms in colonial Canada. One of these, the crusie, was an open pan of sheet-iron, with a handle on one side and a projecting spout on the other. The fuel was animal grease, and the wick was a piece of twisted cotton draped over the lip of the spout. Once the fuel was melted, such lamps burned well, but they were likely to drip grease, and to catch this a second pan was hung beneath the first. Although the name crusie is of Scottish origin, crusie lamps seem to have had their greatest popularity in French Canada.

Another type of pan lamp was brought to Canada by the Pennsylvania Germans. This was the betty lamp. It differed from the crusie in having a sloping trough for the wick, inside the spout of the pan. Any drip from the burning wick would drop inside, rather than outside, the lamp. Most betty lamps had a hinged cover.

True oil lamps were widely used by the more affluent colonists. These burned whale oil, which was readily available and not too expensive up to about 1840. In its simpler form the whale-oil lamp was a glass or metal container, with an opening at the top. Into this opening the burner was plugged or screwed. The burner consisted of a small metal plate, through which one or more metal wick tubes projected. The wicks were pieces of twisted cotton cord. Such a lamp gave more light than a single candle, but required frequent adjustment of the wick, which could be raised or lowered by prying with a small spike through a slot on the side of the wick tube.

Greatly improved whale-oil lamps were introduced towards the close of the eighteenth century, and soon found users in North America. Most of these were based on the invention of Ami Argand, who devised a burner with a tubular wick and a draught of air up the centre. The Argand lamp in various forms persisted through the nineteenth century. Most of the early versions were made in England or France, and imported directly or through the United States. Some were of elegant design, with bronzed ornaments and prism-shaped glass pendants. The great wave of immigrants who came to Canada between 1820 and 1850 included many persons of education and intellectual interests, and for these people a good source of light and a handsome household ornament made a very desirable combination.

During the 1840s the price of whale oil began to rise, and soon it was a luxury for all but the wealthy. People turned to cheaper forms of lamp fuel. The first to be widely used was burning fluid, often erroneously called camphene. This was made by mixing strong alcohol with purified turpentine. It was inexpensive, and when burned in a lamp similar to that used for whale oil, gave a good light without smoke or odour. But it was very likely to explode. During the period of its use, from 1830 to about 1860, burning fluid was the cause of many fires, with considerable loss of life, in both Canada and the United States. Nevertheless, many millions of gallons were made and sold.

Another substitute for whale oil as a lamp fuel was lard. This was easy to obtain and safe to burn, but it is not a liquid at ordinary temperatures. Many ingenious lamps designed to melt the lard, or to make it flow by pressure, were introduced between 1840 and 1860. They were small, unpretentious devices, more suited to kitchen than to parlour, and there are few authentic records of their use in Canada. A more elegant device, the solar lamp, was originally designed for whale oil, but was found to work very well with lard because of the ready transmission of heat from burner to fuel. This was a German invention, and a form of Argand lamp, but most of those that came to Canada were made in Philadelphia. With bronzed font and stem, marble base, and etched-glass shade, the solar lamp was a handsome object, especially if decorated with a ring of glass pendants. The solar lamp took lard as a lamp fuel from the kitchen to the parlour and the dining room.

A new era in domestic lighting began in 1846 with the invention of kerosene. A native of Nova Scotia, Dr Abraham Gesner, first produced this hydrocarbon lamp fuel by distilling coal. Used in a suitable lamp, it was relatively safe and gave a brilliant light. The same substance, under the name of paraffin oil, was made by James Young of Manchester in 1848. It was not until 1854, that kerosene, or coal oil as it was called, appeared on the North American market, and not until 1860, when petroleum became available to replace coal as the source, that it became the dominant lamp fuel. Almost immediately it was widely accepted, and for 20 years it had no rival. Even after the invention of the electric light and the incandescent gas mantle, kerosene retained its popularity in rural Canada until well into the twentieth century.

The cheapness of kerosene permitted the ordinary home-owner to have several lamps, simple models for kitchen and bedroom,

47 Whale-oil lamp burning whale oil

46 Betty lamp, Ontario

48 Lard lamp burning lard

49 Kerosene lamp, *c.* 1860

and ornamental versions for dining room and parlour. These lamps required considerable care. If the wick were raised too high, the flame would produce sooty smoke, which would blacken the inside of the chimney. Cleaning the chimneys with paper, or with soap and water, was a daily household chore. Keeping the wicks well trimmed not only prevented the flame from smoking, but permitted the optimum adjustment for light.

The common type of kerosene lamp in the 1860s consisted of a globular glass vessel or font to hold the fuel, supported on a tubular brass stem and a square plaque of marble for a base. The burner, of brass, screwed into a brass collar on the opening of the font. The wick was ribbon-shaped, and could be raised and lowered in the wick tube by means of a toothed wheel. A dome-shaped cover with a narrow opening for the flame helped to concentrate the air draught. The chimney was high compared with later models, and had only a moderate swelling. It was held on the burner with a set-screw. The more ornamental versions of these lamps had handsome colours or pressed patterns in the glass of the font, and fluted stems. Simple all-glass lamps were also in use, with glass fonts that sat directly on the table, and with glass handles for carrying.

Kerosene had to be manufactured in complex refining plants, and its production became a major industry. It could be obtained only by purchase or barter at the local store, but it was so cheap and so much better than any other lamp fuel that even poor people could afford it. For the farmer working after dark in his barn, complicated but relatively safe kerosene lanterns were soon available.

Illuminating gas, produced by the distillation of coal, became available for domestic lighting early in the nineteenth century. It thus antedated kerosene and was introduced in Montreal and Toronto in the 1840s. In addition to the gas, the distillation produced a number of useful chemicals and a residue of coke that was used in the smelting of iron.

Gas was stored in enormous metal tanks called gasometers. They were like giant cans turned upside down in water. From these the gas was distributed by an elaborate system of pipes. Such a complicated installation restricted gas lighting to larger centres of population. The light from burning gas came from incandescent carbon in the flame. A flat flame gave off more light than a cylindrical flame, so burners were made with a slit-like opening in the tip. Elaborate combinations of glass shades and ornaments were used to make elegant wall and hanging fixtures for the wealthier homes and for public places. The first adequate system of street lighting was by means of gas burners set on posts. The man who lit the flames each evening and turned them off each morning was a familiar figure in Canadian towns.

Improvements in the lighting of homes and public places helped the increase in education, social intercourse, and cultural activities that characterized Canadian society during the nine-teenth century.

8

Food and Drink

Travellers in the colonies that were to be Canada seldom were impressed with the quality of the food. This lack of enthusiasm was usually justified, for their experience was largely confined to inns and hotels. Even by local standards these were bad, both in meals and accommodation. But the Canadian farmer, it was often admitted, did better in both quantity and quality of food than his counterpart in France, England, or Scotland.

THE RAW MATERIALS

Bread, made with wheat flour, was the basic foodstuff almost everywhere. If a public flour mill were nearby, the farmer could have his wheat ground, leaving a portion with the miller as payment. The bran might also be saved for kitchen use, part of it being added to the white flour to produce brown bread for those who preferred it. In more remote communities the farmer might be forced to grind his own flour. This was done in a wooden or iron vessel, using a wooden masher. The product was a very coarse flour, not likely to produce a light bread. A better flour was made in a miniature, hand-powered stone mill called a quern, the use of which is recorded in the Talbot Settlement of Upper Canada and the Red River colony of the future Manitoba.

In preparing corn (maize) for cooking, the kernels were dried, either on or off the cob, dried corn being easier to grind than wheat. Corn meal was used by itself to make a type of bread, or was mixed with wheat flour. Another use for corn was in the dish known as hominy, brought to Canada by American settlers. This was made by boiling the kernels in a weak solution of lye made from wood ashes. When the loosened skin of the kernels was removed, the soft inside made a succulent vegetable dish.

One reason for the extensive use of potatoes in the English-speaking colonies was that they provided a bland counterbalance for the quantities of salt pork that formed the usual meat part of the diet. Mashed potatoes were sometimes mixed with flour dough to produce what was considered a superior kind of bread. Next to potatoes, pumpkins were the most-used vegetable in the English colonies. They were usually boiled and mashed for eating, but were also used as an addition to bread and cake recipes, and for pie fillings.

The French Canadians used large quantities of cabbages and turnips in their cuisine, as well as lesser amounts of onions, green beans, and carrots. Potatoes seem to have been absent from their vegetable list until long after the end of the French régime. The traditional pea soup of French Canada is prepared from field peas and salt pork. Curiously, it is not mentioned in the early books of recipes.

Among the wild plants used as food, rice was the favourite. Unlike the familiar oriental rice, this has long, slender, black grains. It was, and still is, usually harvested by the Indians, from a canoe or boat paddled among the standing plants. The stalks were bent over the rim of the craft with a stick, and the heads beaten with another stick so that the kernels fell into the canoe. Brought to land, the grains were dried over fire, and husked and winnowed like wheat. Wild plants that can serve as boiled greens, such as the dandelion or the lamb's-quarter, are seldom mentioned in the old recipe books. But in New Brunswick a special spring treat was made by picking and boiling the young shoots of the ostrich fern, which, from their coiled shape, are known as fiddleheads. The taste is something between that of spinach and asparagus.

In the early stages of settlement, most fresh meat was obtained from wild game. This was usually the white-tailed deer, the flesh of which when cooked is light-coloured and tender, but sometimes has a slightly bitter 'wild' taste. Farther into the backwoods the moose was the hunter's prize; its meat is dark and coarse-grained but tender and well flavoured. In Newfoundland and the Gaspé peninsula of Quebec there was also the caribou, a kind of reindeer, with light, fine-grained meat. The Red River Settlement, the future Manitoba, had until the 1870s a hinterland with great herds of buffalo (bison). Organized community hunts provided a store of meat as well as hides. Some of this meat was preserved by cutting it into strips and drying it in the sun. It was also the basis of an Indian invention, pemmican, which was made by pounding dried buffalo meat with suet, salt, and berries. The resultant paste was rolled into balls and bound tightly in pieces of buffalo hide. These parcels could be dried to almost rock hardness and apparently would last forever, but soaked and boiled they provided a high-energy food.

The two Canadas (now Quebec and Ontario) shared with the north-eastern United States the fantastic flights of the passenger pigeon, which really darkened the sky. They were an easy prey for the hunter, and were not only shot, but were netted in vast numbers, to be salted in barrels for later consumption. Wild ducks and geese were taken in quantity in the autumn. The tender dark meat of the ruffed grouse, a kind of partridge, was much enjoyed. One form of game that was popular in colonial times but which is no longer eaten is the grey squirrel. It was usually killed with a small-bore rifle, and the flesh preserved by salting.

As previously noted, cattle were raised by the colonists almost exclusively as draught oxen or milk cows. Slaughtering for meat took place only after the animals were no longer able to serve in their original function. Hence the beef available was lean and tough. Another problem with beef was that a single carcass provided more meat than a family could consume before spoilage. Beef was preserved by salting and smoking, as with pork, but the usual solution was for neighbours to co-operate in a slaughtering, each member of the group receiving a portion of the carcass, the animal itself being provided by each member of the group in turn.

Pigs were the commonest domestic source of meat in the colonies. Even a large hog could be slaughtered, cut up, and salted or smoked by a farmer and his son or hired man. Pigs were usually killed by stunning with an axe, then cutting the jugular vein. The carcass was immersed in a tub or barrel of boiling water, after which the hair was scraped from the hide with a dull knife or a special disc-shaped blade on a handle. So many uses were found for the various parts of the pig carcass that the old saying was 'everything is used but the squeal'.

Pork lent itself to several methods of preservation. The commonest technique was salting; it was cheap and relatively simple. The usual method was to soak the cuts of meat in a saturated brine, to which some saltpetre and molasses were added. Soaking was continued for six to eight weeks, with occasional turning. Another way was to spread the pieces of meat where they could drain and rub salt into all sides until the juice ceased to flow. Salt pork was an article of commerce and in both the French and

THE RAW MATERIALS

50 Quern, hand-driven
flour mill

51 Smoke House, Upper
Canada Village,
Morrisburg, Ontario

English periods it was purchased by government as rations for the military or for subsidized settlers. In English Canada it was graded as mess pork (side pieces only), prime mess (also including the hams and shoulders), and prime (all parts packed indiscriminately). In later years the demand was so great that it was imported from the United States (Ohio), where the pigs were allowed to run free, and it was not unusual to find a rifle ball in the meat from this source.

Beef preserved by salting was called 'pickled' rather than 'salt', but the technique was essentially the same as for pork. It was never an article of commerce as was salt pork. Pork or beef preserved with salt required barrels or other containers. By smoking the salted cuts the meat could be stored dry and handled individually. This was done in a small building in which a wood fire could be lit and allowed to smoulder. The cuts were hung over the fire and allowed to absorb the oily constituents of the smoke for several days. Afterwards they were wrapped in cloth and whitewashed for protection against flies. Bacon was made from the sides of pork, salted by the dry method, and smoked.

Sausage-making was another method of preserving meat, especially popular in the German settlements. Often it was a communal operation, taking on the social aspects of a bee. The essential ingredient was fresh pork including both lean and fat parts. But other meats such as beef might be added. The spicing of the sausage, which was the basis of its preservation, varied with local tradition and taste, but pepper and sage were the most widely used. All of the ingredients were chopped or ground

52 Hand-operated sausage stuffer. Paris, Ontario

53 Wooden sausage stuffer

together, perhaps with a semi-circular knife in a wooden bowl. Later, meat-grinding machines became available. The so-called country sausage was simply packed into cloth bags and stored in a cool place until needed, when it was cut into convenient-sized cakes and fried. In the German tradition the sausage meat was stuffed into the cleaned intestine of the pig, the so-called case. In a small operation the stuffing was done with a hand-driven piston in a long funnel. Community sausage making required something larger. One kind of sausage stuffer consisted of a square wooden box, the lid of which could be forced down into it by means of a long lever. On one side of the box, at the bottom, was an opening with a tin spout. With the box filled with sausage meat and one end of the case tied over the spout, it was easy to force the filling into several feet of case. After this was removed from the machine it was tied into convenient lengths for use. Towards the middle of the nineteenth century a cast-iron sausage stuffer became available, much smaller and easier to operate, but using the same principle as the home-made, wooden press.

The Canadian winters provided another means of preserving food—by freezing. Mostly it was game and fish that were kept this way. Sometimes cooked food was frozen, anticipating the prepared dinners of today. In one recipe a barrel was filled with alternate layers of boiled fish and cooked potatoes and the contents frozen. Portions could be chopped out and heated as required.

Chickens, as has been noted, were raised for egg supply. When eggs were abundant they were consumed in large numbers by the hard-working farmers; the favourite way of cooking was frying. Chicken as meat was considered a luxury normally reserved for Sunday dinner. This was the fate of the surplus males in the flock. Geese, in contrast, were kept almost exclusively for meat. A fat goose made a fine main dish for a family dinner, or might be sold at a good profit.

Fish were abundant in all the colonies and formed an important part of the food supply. In the Atlantic region, and especially in Newfoundland, codfish was the staple food. The Newfoundland economy was based on the export of salt codfish, and it was almost a currency there. But it was also part of the popular dish known as fish and brewis (pronounced 'brooz'). For this the codfish was soaked to remove part of the salt, then boiled with potatoes and ship's biscuit ('hardtack'). The mixture was flavoured with pork dripping and topped off with pieces of fried-out pork rind, called scruncheons.

The magnificent Atlantic salmon was either cooked fresh or preserved by smoking. In Nova Scotia the favourite fish was herring, salted and dried. Eels, abundant in the St Lawrence drainage, were prepared by boiling and pickling. Other interior fish used for food were the whitefish, trout, bass and pike. Less common but highly prized was the sturgeon.

Wild fruits provided a few luxuries for the early settlers. Earliest in the year were the strawberries, small by modern standards, but very sweet. Later in the year, wild raspberries could be gathered in abundance. Burned-over areas yielded rich crops of blueberries, which were harvested with a kind of scoop having a comb-shaped lip. In the swamps, large juicy cranberries were abundant. Newfoundland had its special favourites, such as the bake-apple, a raspberry-like fruit that makes up as a delicious jam, and partridge berries, small red berries growing close to the ground in swampy places. In the far western Red River Settlement there were also special wild fruits. The Saskatoon or serviceberry grows on a small tree or shrub; it resembles a blueberry in appearance but has a very different flavour. Excellent for jam or pie filling, it was also the berry that was added to the buffalo-meat paste in making pemmican. Very different is the choke-cherry, a small, black, cluster-forming berry with a large pit. Choke-cherries are too astringent to be enjoyed raw, but can be boiled to make a sweet syrup. Closely related to the choke-cherry is the wild plum, once abundant in the Canadas and in the Red River valley. It is a small, yellowish fruit, with a flavour unlike that of the domestic plum.

Of all cultivated fruits, apples were the most widely grown and used. They were eaten raw, or cooked fresh, in season, but their most important use was as dried fruit, in which form they were available all year. Preparation of the apples for drying became a social event, the 'pairing bee'. This was an opportunity for the young men and girls to work together, and one way to gain prestige was to bring a peeling device more ingenious and efficient than the others. Most of these peelers consisted of a shaft mounted horizontally on bearings across the end of a board. At one end of the shaft was a two-pronged fork to skewer the apple. At the other end was a crank to turn the shaft. As the apple was turned with one hand, a knife blade was held against it with the other. By incorporating a pulley drive, and using special peeling knives, the operation could be accelerated. But the competitive spirit sometimes led to carelessness in peeling, and in keeping the apples clean. Coring and slicing was the task of the girls. The slices, like large washers, were dried on screens in the sun, or threaded on string and hung from wall to wall in the kitchen. When needed, they were soaked and boiled, making an excellent apple sauce. About the middle of the nineteenth century, patented apple peelers of iron, using screws or gears, and with built-in knives, made the peeling swift and simple. Gradually the social gatherings associated with this task diminished, until the paring bee became only a memory of the 'good old days'.

The German settlers from Pennsylvania introduced the making of apple butter, and this too became a social event. Apple butter is simply a thick apple sauce, worked well for smoothness, and flavoured with brown sugar, cloves, and cinnamon, and perhaps with some pumpkin added. Community apple-butter making was done in the open, the apples being stewed in a large copper pot over a fire. Besides the peeling, coring, and slicing of the apples, participants had to take turns at stirring the mix, without which it would quickly burn on the bottom.

For sweetening, the early settlers in the Canadas made extensive use of maple syrup and maple sugar, the preparation of which is described in chapter 11. In the Atlantic colonies no such native sweetener was at hand, and large amounts of cane sugar and molasses were brought from the West Indies, in exchange for salted fish. These materials came in giant barrels called puncheons,

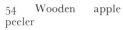

54 Wooden apple peeler

55 Mennonite ladies preparing apples for drying. Black Creek Pioneer Village

56 Stirring apple butter with a rotary paddle. Cedar Grove, Ontario

holding something like 100 gallons. Unloading and transporting them were major operations. The sugar, which was of the brown variety, and moist, became very compact, and was dug out as required with a sugar auger, a kind of giant corkscrew. When all of the solid sugar was removed, there was a dividend of sweet syrup called treacle at the bottom, much prized for pouring over porridge and pancakes.

White sugar, when available, came in the form of a tall, narrow cone called a sugar loaf. It took this shape from the funnel in which the manufacturer placed the freshly crystallized sugar to drain off the residual treacle. To use the loaf, the housewife snipped off portions with special, short-bladed shears. Loaf sugar was expensive, and was used mainly in tea.

Vinegar, at the other end of the taste scale, was much used for pickling. It was either imported, or made from apple cider. Another source was the late run of maple sap, which was low in sugar. Onions were the most popular pickles. The whole onions were soaked in salted water, scalded, and placed in jars with vinegar. Pickled cucumbers and melons were also prepared.

57 Sugar auger

58 Reconstructed fire-place of the Halfway House, Black Creek Pioneer Village, Ontario

COOKING

Until about 1840, and later in some areas, the kitchen fireplace was the principal means of cooking. The Loyalists and the German settlers built fireplaces with the oven as a chamber in the front wall, to one side of the main opening. In Lower Canada, and parts of the Atlantic colonies, the oven was usually separate from the fireplace. The French-Canadian outdoor oven was a characteristic feature of the farm yard, and some examples are still in use. It is a vaulted chamber of fired clay, supported on a stone or wooden foundation, and usually with a wooden roof overhead. There is an iron door in front and a smoke vent in the rear. With both indoor and outdoor ovens the method of heating was the same. A fire was built or introduced in the chamber; when the walls were hot enough the fire was shovelled and swept out and the loaves introduced. Where large amounts of bread had to be baked, as at an inn, a separate bakehouse was used, with its own fireplace and oven.

Much fireplace cooking was done in pots suspended over the fire. At an early stage in household development the settler might fix a stout green pole horizontally in the fireplace vent, and suspend his pots from this on chains. Sooner or later the pole would dry and char, perhaps with disastrous results. The crane was a much safer and convenient means of support. It was an iron bar, shaped like an inverted letter L. The vertical arm was set into iron rings in the wall of the fireplace. The horizontal arm could be swung from a position over the fire to well outside the fireplace, where the pots could be attached or removed.

Often the crane was set high above the fire, and the level of the pot adjusted by means of a trammel. This was a saw-like device, each 'tooth' of the blade serving as a stop at which the trammel could be set, and so providing a series of heights at which the pot might be hung.

Pots were of cast iron, with or without lids. Some were shallow, with flat bottoms, and served both for stewing and frying. Others were deep, with round bottoms for convenience in cleaning. Round-bottomed pots usually had three short legs for support when set on floor or table. Double boilers were improvised by hanging the pot inside a larger pot with boiling water. Even the modern pressure cooker was anticipated. A heavy iron pot with a clamped lid had a device for controlling the escape of steam; when this was partly closed, steam pressure inside the pot was increased and the time of cooking shortened.

Frying was done on flat pans hung from the crane, or on 'spiders', which were skillets with three long legs. Broiling involved searing the meat surface to seal in the juices. It was done on a grid iron, a grating of iron bars on legs. In more sophisticated grid irons the bars were narrow troughs, which opened at the handle end into a shallow cup. Juices from the broiling meat ran down the troughs and collected in the cup, where they could be spooned out and used to baste the meat.

Roasting was not much different from broiling, but was done with large cuts or with a whole pig. The usual method was to skewer the meat on an iron rod, which was mounted on supports in a horizontal position. When this device was set in front of the fire, and the rod turned by a handle or a pulley, the meat was uniformly exposed to the heat. This arrangement was called a spit. In large kitchens, especially in French Canada, the spit was connected by pulley ropes to a treadmill or a rotating cage, in which a dog supplied the motive power for turning. The clock jack, an English device, was more characteristic of Upper Canada. It was a brass cylinder containing a powerful spring motor. At the lower end was a hook, and when the spring was wound the motor turned the hook back and forth in opposite circles. The clock jack was hung from the rim of the fireplace, above and in front of the fire. A joint of meat, attached to the hook, was turned one way, then the other, and uniformly roasted. The name of this device comes from the old name for the scullery boy, 'Jack'.

The reflector oven was introduced in the early 1800s from the United States. It was a half cylinder of shiny tin, mounted so that the long axis was horizontal, with the open side facing the fire. A skewer from one end to the other held the meat in position, and when this was turned the meat was exposed not only to the direct heat of the fire, but also to that reflected from the shiny wall of the oven. Reflector ovens were also made with the walls in the form of two flat sheets mounted at 45° to the horizontal, and meeting at right angles along the rear. It thus formed a kind of trough set on its edge. Flanges across the ends supported a pan or tray on which biscuits or pies were placed, to bake from the heat reflected down from the upper wall and up from the lower one. Food baked this way was well cooked but did not have the appetizing brown coating produced by true oven baking.

The so-called Dutch oven is presumed to have been brought to Canada by the Pennsylvania Germans. It was a shallow, heavy iron pot with a flat bottom and a tight-fitting lid. Biscuits or bread were baked in this pot by covering it with live coals in the fireplace. Food baked in this manner was good, and the operation relatively quick.

The kitchen fireplace had other interesting accessories. Bread was usually toasted on a long-handled fork, but some households had a special toasting frame. This was set on the floor in front of the fire, and could be revolved to expose both sides of the slices. Tall, circular trivets were used for supporting pots and pans both on and off the fire. The oven on the side of the fireplace could be used for meat, but it was intended primarily for bread baking. There were two ways of heating the oven. It could be filled with live coals from the fireplace, or a fire of specially cut wood pieces could be kindled in the oven chamber. After several hours the oven was emptied, either with a shovel, or by pushing the ashes through a hole into the fireplace. The loaves of dough were then introduced, either as rounded balls on a greased metal plate, or in round or rectangular bread pans of iron. The metal door of the oven was closed and the bread left to bake overnight. The outdoor oven of French Canada was always heated with its own fire. Such ovens were safer to operate, there being no danger of fire from scattered embers, and in summer they made it unnecessary to have a fire in the house. But even with a wooden roof they must have been inconvenient to use in wet or cold weather.

Although stoves had come into use for heating houses in the

59 Clock jack　　　60 Reconstructed kitchen of about 1863, showing dry
sink and dish rack, also cooking stove

eighteenth century, it was not until about 1840 that the cooking
stove began to displace the fireplace as the culinary altar. Early
kitchen stoves, many of them made in Canadian foundries, were
of two types. The so-called range fitted into the existing fireplace.
In its more elaborate form it had a firebox, ovens, and warming
chambers, all arranged ingeniously to make the most of radiating
heat and circulating smoke. The separate stove was more usual,
and was set in front of the bricked-up fireplace, into which the
stove pipe was inserted. The firebox was low, with a door in front
for adding fuel and removing ashes. Cooking was done on the
top of the firebox, with or without the 'lids' in place. The oven
was a box-like structure set over the rear of the firebox. Hot air
and smoke from the fire passed between the double walls of the
oven on their way to the stove pipe. The arrangement was
efficient in the use of heat and the low level of the cooking surface,
which necessitated much stooping, was perhaps acceptable to a
cook accustomed to bending over a fire. More convenient cook
stoves, with the firebox beside the oven, and a much higher stove
top, were introduced in the 1870s.

Baking was just the last step in bread making. The more
difficult part was the 'raising' of the dough. This involved
impregnating the mixture of flour and water with minute bubbles
of carbon dioxide ('fixed air'), which gave the essential porosity
and 'lightness' to the baked bread. There were three ways of
raising dough: by fermentation of the flour starch with yeast, by
the chemical reaction of sodium bicarbonate with the lactic acid
of sour milk, and by the reaction of baking powder (sodium

95

bicarbonate and tartaric acid) when it was added to wet dough. The yeast method was nearly always used for bread, the others being more common for biscuits, cakes, and pancakes. Getting a good strain of yeast was not easy, and once obtained, it was preserved by keeping a portion of each batch from one dough-making to the next. The barm or yeast liquor was prepared by boiling hops or potato paste, and priming the cooled fluid with some of the old yeast. The mixture was allowed to stand for a day or two so that the yeast could develop.

Dough making was a strenuous manual operation. Small amounts were made on a flour-dusted table top, but large batches were prepared in a trough-shaped box. To the heap of sifted flour, water and yeast were added a little at a time, and the mixture worked to the consistency of a viscid mass. Some recipes called for the addition of pulverized boiled potato, or of bran, or corn meal. A little salt or sugar might be added, to suit the taste. Working or kneading of the dough to get rid of lumps and mix the yeast uniformly was done with various motions: rolling, folding, squeezing, punching, and even throwing down hard on the table. The kneaded dough was then placed in a covered bowl, or in the dough box with a lid, and left to rise for an hour or two in a warm place. Some cooks kneaded and raised the dough a second time before baking. This gave a more uniform porosity.

Travellers in both French and English Canada complained about the sour taste of the bread. This probably was the result of using poor yeast. Where there were breweries, it was not difficult to obtain a good yeast culture. By the middle of the nineteenth century, dry yeast was available in grocers' shops.

'Salt-rising' bread was made without benefit of yeast. A mixture of salted water and flour was set in a warm place; after three or four hours it would begin to effervesce. Promptly it was mixed with additional flour to make a dough, which was allowed to rise in the usual manner before baking. This kind of bread had a peculiar flavour that some people found objectionable.

Various kinds of biscuits and cakes were made using baking powder or baking soda. Before these materials were available by purchase, a substitute called salaeratus was made by treating 'pearl ash' (potassium hydroxide) with 'fixed air' (carbon dioxide) to produce potassium bicarbonate. The Scottish term 'bannock' was applied to bread made with salaeratus or baking powder, and was usually cooked in a Dutch oven or the reflector.

Porridge of various sorts was widely used in the English-speaking colonies. Mostly it was the Scottish version, made with ground oats, but wheat and corn were also used. Corn porridge was called supporne, and had the additional merit that when cold it was solid enough to be sliced. These slices, fried, were much esteemed by settlers of American origin. They were very good when well browned, tasting like fried potatoes.

The pioneers ate to satisfy hunger and to provide energy for their heavy labour. As the settlements matured, people thought of improving the flavour of their food with herbs and spices. In the early nineteenth century many of the immigrants were of middle-class origin, and they helped to create a demand for more sophisticated flavours. The growing of herbs became a widespread practice. Perhaps the easiest to grow was summer savoury. Fresh or dried, it gave a delicious flavour to meat, stew, and soup. Mint grew almost too readily, but gave a tang to gravy and sauces. Sage was the herb traditionally used in dressing.

Among the imported spices, nutmeg was probably the favourite, judging by the number and variety of nutmeg graters that have survived. Other spices used were cloves and cinnamon. Black pepper was used in cooking; its presence on the table with salt came later.

Fruits were eaten raw in season but were harvested mostly for preserving in some form. When sugar was available in good quantity, jams and jellies were made, and glass jars for holding the preserves were early objects of import or manufacture. On established farms the 'preserving time' was a regular autumn event, and housewives practised good aseptic techniques by boiling jars and contents long before the role of micro-organisms in decomposition was understood. Plums, both wild and cultivated, were 'made up' from the earliest days of settlement; cherries and peaches came later. Some of the wild fruits, such as raspberries and bake-apples, were preserved as jam.

DAIRY PRODUCTS

As noted, the keeping of cows in colonial times was mainly for milk production, and especially for butter. In these days of large dairy farms, with electric milking machines, and elaborate processing and marketing of the products, the routine of handling a few cows, of daily milking, and of churning the butter, seem like the customs of another world.

For the first day or two after the milk cow 'came in', the calf was allowed to suckle, as the early milk contains much cellular debris and is not fit for human consumption. Milking was usually done in the barn or shed, where the cow could be tethered in a stall. Although milking by European tradition was the task of women ('milk-maids'), on Canadian farms it was usually done by men or boys. The milker sat on the right side of the cow, on a three-legged stool or perhaps just a block of wood. Grasping two of the four teats, one in each hand, he squeezed each alternately with a pulling action, directing the streams of milk into a pail steadied between his legs. The final operation was 'stripping', pulling down on the teat between thumb and fingers to get the last of the milk. A good cow in those days would provide enough milk at one milking to fill a medium-sized pail.

The fresh milk was cooled as quickly as possible, in a root cellar or in a spring. It was then placed in shallow pans of tin, crockery, or glass, and kept at a cool temperature. In about 36 hours the cream rose to the surface, and was skimmed off with a shallow scoop or a large spoon. The skimmed milk was fed to the calf, or used in cooking. Whole milk was drunk in quantities by French-Canadian farmers, but in English Canada it was used mainly for feeding infants.

The cream was kept in a moderately cool place for 'ripening', and in a few hours the bacteria normally present in milk converted the sugar into lactic acid. When fully 'soured', the cream was ready for churning. The typical churn of the early colonists was a kind of keg, narrow and high, and tapering slightly from bottom to top. In the nineteenth century, crockery churns were available; they were shaped like a small barrel. In either form they had a hole in the lid for the handle of the dasher. At the lower end of this rod, inside the churn, were two pieces of wood set at right angles to form a simple cross. In use the churn was partly filled with sour cream and the dasher moved up and down vigorously. Churning by hand was a slow, tedious operation, usually assigned to the children.

Much ingenuity was expended to devise a churn that was easier to operate and faster in producing butter. The box churn was a rectangular or cylindrical container, with a shaft extending through it horizontally. Inside the box the shaft bore four paddles, and on the outside, at one end, a crank with handle. Partly filled with cream, and with the lid closed, the box churn was operated by turning the shaft and paddles by means of the external crank.

Agitating the cream by shaking, rather than by impact of dasher or paddle, was another way of making butter. A box mounted on a pivot, with a handle for rocking back and forth, was an effective churn. Another was a sheet-metal cylinder about three feet long, with pointed ends. This could be hung from the ceiling on two ropes, and rocked end to end with moderate effort. In later years the barrel churn appeared, a stout cask mounted on a frame, and capable of being rapidly spun or rocked by means of a handle or foot pedal. A complicated wooden device with a seat, and with handles and foot pedals, was coupled to the dasher of the vertical churn. The operator, by pulling and pushing as if rowing a boat, produced vigorous strokes of the dasher. In churns with a rotary action, the motive power was sometimes provided by a dog tread-mill.

61 *Above:* Dasher churn

62 Churns; two swinging churns in front, a rocker churn in rear, and a small box churn on the right

63 *Right:* Dog tread-mill

However the agitation was produced, the impact of the fat globules against each other caused them to coalesce, producing masses of solid butter. This was removed from the churn by hand. Most of the watery part of the cream remained in the churn. This buttermilk was poured or drawn off, and when cooled, was enjoyed as a refreshing drink. There was still a lot of liquid in the butter. After washing with cold water, the next stage was 'working'. The lumps of butter were placed in a large wooden bowl, and pressed repeatedly with the bottom of a slightly concave scoop called a butter paddle. Salt, and perhaps a little saltpetre (potassium nitrate) would be worked into the butter in this operation.

A more elaborate butter-working device was in the form of a triangular table, the top sloping to the point of the triangle, and the sides provided with low walls. The working tool was a wooden bar, something like a rolling pin, but with a number of flat sides instead of a smooth cylindrical surface. One end of the tool was pivoted at the lower end of the table, the other provided with a handle. Butter placed on the table was squeezed back and forth by rolling the tool from side to side in the arc of a circle. The squeezed-out liquid flowed down the slope of the table and out an opening at the narrow end.

Butter made from the milk of cows that had eaten wild onions in the woods had a strong, objectionable taste. Chopped turnips in the winter diet of the cows might have a similar effect. These taints could be neutralized to some extent by using more saltpetre. In winter, when green fodder was not available, the butter was pale in colour, almost like lard, and some people found this appearance objectionable. It was changed by adding a little vegetable colouring, such as an infusion of goldenrod flowers prepared in the autumn with this requirement in mind. By mid-nineteenth century, small bottles of butter colouring were available at the local store.

Cheese making was a more elaborate operation than butter making, and had to be done in large quantities if the effort was to be worth while. As the settlements expanded, community cheese factories were set up, and eventually cheese making became a major industry in areas favourable to dairy farming. As dairy farms became larger, they might go into cheese making for themselves, as the product had a good market.

Most Canadian cheese was of the cheddar variety. It was made by curdling whole or skimmed milk with rennet, which comes from the stomach lining of a young calf. In later years, prepared rennet could be purchased, but formerly there were many home recipes for making this important agent. The stomach lining of a freshly killed calf was dried and brushed clean. It could be preserved by salting. In use, a portion was soaked in water and the liquid added to the milk. In a few minutes the milk began to curdle, separating into solid curd and liquid whey. After the whey was drained off, the curd was worked in various ways, such as breaking or cutting, depending on the method of the cheese maker. Some souring might be permitted, as lactic acid helped to solidify the curd. The final step was pressing, to remove the last of the liquid and produce a solid block of cheese. A simple method was to wrap the curd in cloth and place it in a stout basket under a lid weighted with a stone.

More sophisticated cheese presses consisted of a wooden frame supporting a stout vertical screw. At the upper end of the screw shaft was a handle, on the lower end a flat face to press on the lid of the cheese container. Another type of press had a complicated

64 Butter bowl and paddle

65 Butter worker

66 Cheese presses: screw press on the left, lever press in centre

system of levers to obtain the vertical pressure. After the cheese blocks had been compressed as much as possible, they were wrapped in cloth and allowed to stand for a few weeks. Most Canadian cheese was eaten during the year that it was produced. It was long after colonial times that the demand for well-aged cheese justified setting up the necessary storage facilities.

So-called cottage cheese was made without rennet. The milk was allowed to sour until curds were formed. These were strained in a cloth until firm. They were then beaten to smoothness, adding cream, salt, pepper, or onion, to taste. Cottage cheese was only for domestic consumption, as it did not remain edible for long without refrigeration.

BEVERAGES

Most colonial farms had a spring or well from which clear, cold water could be obtained. So the common thirst quencher was a 'dipper' of cold water. Perhaps this was the beginning of the North American custom of serving water with meals, which visitors have found worthy of comment.

For the French colonists the traditional drink was wine, but the *vin ordinaire* of France became an expensive luxury when transported to America. Only the wealthy merchant or seignior could afford it, and they preferred the richer wines of Spain or Portugal. Some effort was made to produce wine from Canadian vineyards, or even from the wild grapes, a more acidic fruit, but this was never very successful. In Upper Canada, parts of which proved to be more suitable for grape growing, the English-speaking colonists had no tradition of wine making.

In the seventeenth century the government of New France tried to encourage beer-drinking by establishing breweries, but even though northern France had a beer-drinking tradition, beer did not become a popular French-Canadian drink until large-scale breweries were established in the nineteenth century. The English-speaking colonists, who might have been expected to prefer beer and ale, brewed very little, and only in the taverns of large settlements were these beverages usually available. Various substitutes were tried, such as spruce beer, made from the tender twigs of that tree, and maple beer, from the late, weak sap fermented with hops.

Of all the native beverages, apple cider was the most popular, especially in the German settlements. The essential equipment for cider making was a press to squeeze the juice out of the apples.

This varied from a small table model for family use to a large machine in a community cider mill, where farmers could bring their apples for pressing, leaving a portion of the juice as payment.

In such large establishments the apples were pulverized by grinding or chopping. The resultant pulp was then placed in the press, with layers of straw alternating with layers of pulp. Pressure applied by means of a large vertical screw squeezed the juice out of the pulp into pails, from which it was transferred into barrels.

Fermentation of the cider had to be carefully controlled or it would produce vinegar. The process was stopped at the proper moment by moving the barrels to a cool place, not too difficult to find in the late autumn. Fermented cider could be distilled to produce a kind of brandy, but a strong drink could also be produced by freezing the cider in the barrel. The alcohol, having a lower freezing point, remained as a liquid 'core' in the centre of the ice, and could be drawn or dipped off. The liquor, known as apple-jack, compared with whiskey in alcoholic content.

In French Canada the popular strong drink was brandy (*eau de vie*), but as this, like wine, had to be imported, it was too expensive for common use. Much of the brandy brought to Canada was used to stimulate the fur trade with the Indians, a practice greatly deplored by the missionary priests, but considered necessary to meet the competition of the Dutch and English traders, for whom rum was the inducement to trade.

In the Atlantic colonies, rum imported from the West Indies was relatively cheap, and was drunk in large quantities. By the time it reached Upper Canada, rum was too expensive to meet the competition of whiskey, which was distilled from the fermented mash of rye, barley, or wheat. During the early part of the nineteenth century, distilleries became almost as common as flour mills in this colony, and much more profitable in spite of the low charge for their product. One reason for this development was that the farming methods of the time produced a large proportion of dirty or frozen grain, which was good enough for distilling, and which could be purchased at very low cost. Whiskey-drinking in Upper Canada became like beer-drinking or wine-drinking in other countries, and the widespread drunkenness that resulted was commented upon by many visitors from abroad. Eventually the influence of the churches and temperance societies, as well as the improved standard of living, reduced the excesses, if not the custom, of whiskey drinking. Improved farming methods, including mechanization, cut off the supply of waste grain with a resultant increase in the price of whiskey and a reduction in the number of distilleries.

Tea-drinking was brought to Canada by both the Loyalists and the immigrants from England. Both black and green tea were used. But tea was never popular in the French or German parts of Canada, and it was strange even to the Irish immigrants. Tea was a fashionable drink in the homes of the English-speaking officials and merchants, and 'taking tea' was an occasion that called for fine china and silver service. There is a tradition that it was considered polite in the 'old days' to drink from the saucer, but eighteenth-century records indicate that such a practice was regarded as ill-mannered.

Coffee was the popular drink of the Pennsylvania Germans and other post-Loyalist immigrants from the United States. It was imported from 'Arabia' in the form of green beans. Households had their own coffee roasters, which were metal cans with a lidded opening on one side and a long rod extending through the middle. Such containers, supported on a permanent form, or pivoted on temporary uprights in front of the fire could be turned like a spit while the coffee beans roasted uniformly. When cooking stoves became common, the coffee roaster reappeared as a flat iron pot with a lid, of the right diameter to fit into the stove opening. A shaft projecting up through the lid had a handle on top and paddle-like blades inside. Rotating these paddles produced uniform roasting of the beans without burning.

Even when roasted coffee beans became available in the shops, most households still used their own coffee grinders. No doubt coffee was originally ground in some sort of mortar, but by the eighteenth century mechanical coffee mills were in wide use. The usual mill consisted of a wooden box, with a drawer to catch the grindings. On the top of the box was a circular opening, with a brass funnel and an iron disc or cone with cutting edges. Beans placed in the funnel were caught by the rotating cutter and crushed as they worked their way down. Another model was mounted on the wall, and the ground coffee caught in a glass jar screwed to the bottom of the grinding mechanism. Eventually it became the custom to buy the roasted coffee beans at the shop and have them ground there. The large red or black coffee mill with its two fly-wheels became almost a symbol of the old-time general store.

Tea and coffee were expensive by settler's standards, and local plants were used as substitutes. Some of these usages were learned from the Indians. The small flowering shrub known as New Jersey tea was one of these plants; the tender leaves were dried and infused, as with the imported tea, but the resultant brew was not liked by all who tried it. A tea-like drink was also made from the bark of the sassafras tree. In the backwoods a popular substitute for tea was made from a small creeping plant called Labrador tea, which grows in swampy places. The flavour was said to be resinous, but it was widely used in the early lumber camps.

TABLE MANNERS

What constitutes good table manners, like other forms of etiquette, varies with country and with time. The essential part is an accepted ritual that takes the emphasis away from the physical aspects of eating and drinking. But in the early colonial settlements there was an urgency to get on with the work at hand, together with a lack of the accoutrements of gracious living. In short, colonial table manners were usually bad.

In French Canada the governing officials, the seigniors, and the townspeople of means, consciously strove to maintain the gracious traditions of their homeland. Description of a formal dinner in a manor tells of fine linen, bright silver, and sparkling glass, and of politeness and formality of table manners to match. But a curious feature was the absence of knives from the settings. Each guest brought his own, and those of the ladies came in decorated leather cases. Gracious manners in the upper-class homes set an example for others. The typical habitant home had a good supply of steel forks and pewter spoons and plates. However unsophisticated the family might be, their table manners were dignified by simple religious observance and by respect for the *père de famille*.

In the English-speaking colonies the variations in table manners were extreme. The Loyalists brought with them the customs of the American colonies, and these were reinforced by later American immigrants. These customs were not all the British government officials and European visitors thought admirable, but they included a germ of politeness based on the principle that everyone at the table should get his fair share. The wave of immigration from the British Isles in the first half of the nineteenth century brought to Canada many people of education and culture, but it also brought the English factory worker, the Scottish crofter, and the Irish potato-farmer. These people, however admirable they might be, had little tradition of gracious living, and their background, combined with the North American ideas of individual freedom that even the Loyalists cherished, sometimes produced a boorishness that was blamed on 'Yankee republicanism', but which was often only a sign of insecurity.

In the poorer homes, where table equipment was limited, food was served in bowls, from which each person helped himself. The knife was the principal instrument of eating, more important even than the spoon, while the fork, a three-tined version with a wooden handle, was almost redundant. In the public eating places Canadian manners appeared at their worst. For the guests, the main object seemed to be to eat as much as possible as quickly as possible. For the management, the least service required the better. This, together with greasy, unpalatable food, and a careless attitude towards cleanliness, made eating in public places almost intolerable for persons accustomed to polite manners, clean service, and good food.

9

Textiles

The art of weaving, that is, of producing a pliable protective material by the interlacing of strands of animal or vegetable fibres, had reached a high state of development in Europe by the time the first colonies were established in northern North America. The fibres for weaving were derived from the wool of sheep, the stems of the flax plant, and the seed fibres of the cotton plant. The early colonists brought all three types of textiles with them, and throughout colonial history they or their descendants imported large quantities from Europe and later from the United States. But the production of woollen and linen fabrics soon became an important part of domestic economy, later to be expanded into a textile industry. Cotton, of course, could not be grown in such a northern climate, and its use as a fabric was restricted to those who could afford the imported material.

WOOL

Many attempts were made by Canadian settlers to raise sheep, but these animals were particularly vulnerable to the attacks of wolves, and they were not so able as cattle to forage in the northern winters. But the colonists persisted, so important was it to have a source of wool, and they succeeded to the extent that the spinning and weaving of wool became a widespread household activity.

Sheep were sheared in the spring, when the heavy coat of wool was no longer needed for protection. Cutting free the fleece was done with a kind of scissors, and the expert shearer kept the mass of wool in one piece without nipping the sheep. Sometimes the sheep were very dirty, and had to be washed in a stream or pond before shearing. More often, however, the cleaning of the separated fleece was by means of soap and water.

After the fleece had been washed it still contained bits of foreign matter, such as burrs and twigs, and these had to be picked out by hand. If there was much wool to be picked, it might be done by bringing in the neighbours for a wool-picking bee. After the final picking, the next stage was to replace the natural wool oil removed by the washing. Grease from the kitchen was commonly used for this purpose, and was worked into the mass of wool by hand.

Before the wool could be spun into yarn, it had to be carded. In this operation the fibres of the wool were combed so as to lie approximately parallel. The 'cards' were plaques of wood about five inches by seven. From one edge a handle projected. One surface of the plaque was covered with leather, from which a thick array of wires projected about a quarter of an inch. In some cards the wires were hook-shaped, in others just straight little teeth. In using the cards a tuft of wool was placed on one of them, and then, one in each hand, the cards were pulled across each other. When the fibres had been combed out thoroughly, the wool was rolled into a tassel and removed. Carding was a slow and tiring task, usually delegated to the children. Among the earliest of textile factories were carding mills, usually operated by water power; here the wool was cleaned and carded mechanically. The carded wool, less a portion retained for payment, was returned to the owner for spinning.

Wool was usually spun into yarn on the large wheel. The base of this was a narrow, three-legged table about 18 inches high at one end and a foot high at the other. At the lower end, two uprights supported a large wheel, about three feet in diameter, with a flat outer rim. From this rim a cord extended to a pulley wheel or whorl on the spindle. The spindle was a steel spike about eight inches long, held loosely in a horizontal position by two leather loops from small wooden posts called maidens. Spinning-wheels in which the spindle was driven directly from the big wheel were characteristic of the Atlantic colonies. In Lower and Upper Canada there was usually another shaft mounted above the spindle; this had a small pulley wheel for the cord from the big wheel, and a larger pulley wheel connected by a short loop of cord to the pulley wheel on the spindle. The object of this indirect drive was to increase the spindle's speed of rotation.

The wool wheel was operated from the standing position. The spinner twisted a wisp of the carded wool onto the spindle, then gave the big wheel a flip by hand or with a stick. As the spindle whirled, the spinner fed more wool onto the rapidly twisting yarn,

67 Carding boards and raw wool

68 Walking wheel for spinning wool

69 Spindle mechanism on walking wheel

backing away as the length of the twisted part increased. On reaching a distance of about a yard, or when the momentum of the big wheel had run down, the spinner stepped to a position close to the wheel, gave it another flip, and allowed the length of spun yarn to wind itself onto the spindle.

When the coil of yarn on the spindle became so large as to interfere with the spinning, it was unwound onto some other device, usually a 'niddy-noddy'. This was a wooden rod about 15 inches long, with other pieces about a foot long attached to the end at right angles. The shape was like that of two letter Ts, one right-side-up, the other upside-down, but the cross-arms of the Ts were at right angles to each other. Holding the niddy-noddy at the middle, the spinner drew off the yarn from the spindle with a kind of figure-eight motion, stretching it diagonally from one arm to the other. This stretching helped to eliminate irregularities in the twist.

The wool was transferred from the niddy-noddy or the spindle to some form of reel. In one familiar type the reel was mounted vertically. On its shaft a spiral groove was carved, and in this the

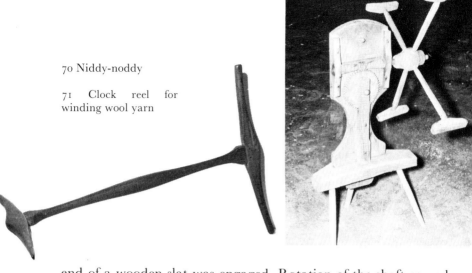

end of a wooden slat was engaged. Rotation of the shaft caused the slat to move from one end of the spiral to the other, where it would be released to fly back with a loud click. This device was called a clock-reel. Various numbers of revolutions might be indicated by the click, but the common number was 40. This indicated that 80 yards of yarn had been wound on the reel. Seven clicks of the reel meant that a skein of yarn had been wound, a common unit in using wool. For knitting the skein was unwound from the reel by hand into the convenient ball. For weaving it was taken off by winding onto a bobbin. This was usually done on a winding-wheel, a device somewhat like a spinning-wheel but with the pulley turning a bobbin instead of a spindle.

Spinning with the wool-wheel involved constant stepping back and forth, and the device was sometimes called a walking-wheel. The distance travelled could add up to miles. In some old houses the site of the wheel was marked by a foot-worn area on the floor. About the middle of the nineteenth century a wool-wheel was invented in which the spindle was mounted on a swinging arm, operated by a foot pedal. The motion of the arm, first away, then back, took the place of the spinner's walking.

LINEN

Linen, the other textile made in colonial Canada, was woven from the fibres of the flax plant. Linen-making was not as widely practised as woollen-cloth production, but was more common in French Canada than in other parts. The flax grown in colonial times was a long-stemmed variety unlike modern flax, which is grown for its seed. Flax was planted in June and harvested in late August. The plants were harvested by pulling, not cutting. First step in the preparation of linen was to separate the seed capsules from the stems. This was done by pulling the heads through a heavy iron or wooden comb, called a ripple. Originally the seeds were saved only for future planting, but later they were pressed to yield the valuable linseed oil. The flax stalks were then soaked in water for several days; this step, called retting, broke down the central, more woody core of the stems. Sometimes the retting was done by spreading the pulled plants in the field, where dew and rain would accomplish the same result as soaking.

The partly-rotted woody core of the stems now had to be broken. This was done on a device called a brake. In its simplest form it consisted of two parallel blades of wood mounted on four legs. At one end, another blade was pivoted edge down. This middle blade could be swung in a vertical arc, and when down it fitted between the two fixed blades. The flax stalks were laid across the two fixed blades and the middle blade swung down forcibly. This operation, repeated many times, broke up the core of the stems but did not harm the fibres. It was more usual for the brake to have three fixed blades and two pivoted ones.

The next step in the preparation of linen was called scutching; it served to remove the fragments of core left by the brake. The flax stems were laid over the edge of a vertically mounted board, and struck downward glancing blows with a scutching blade, a wooden tool shaped like a butcher's knife. Up to this point the

72 Flax being pulled and laid out for retting. Black Creek Pioneer Village, Ontario

73 Flax brake

work of preparing the flax was strenuous, and was almost always performed by men. Now the women took over. The tangled fibres of the flax, more or less free of other matter, were straightened by means of a device called a heckle or hetchel. It was an array of sharp spikes projecting upward from a board. In use, the board was secured to a table, and handfuls of the flax fibres were drawn repeatedly through the spikes. Design of heckles varied greatly from one area to another. French Canadians had one design, Germans from Pennsylvania another, and so on. By mounting the spikes at one end of a long board, it was possible to hold the heckle steady by sitting on the other end.

The heckled flax was called tow. It was folded into hanks and kept in this form until it could be spun. The spinning-wheel used for flax was much smaller and more sophisticated than the large wool-wheel. A good operator could spin wool yarn on a flax-wheel, but it was impossible to spin flax on a wool-wheel. The flax-wheel was turned by means of a foot pedal, connected by a stiff rod to a little crank on the axle of the wheel. This made it possible to spin while sitting down. A double-looped cord connected the wheel to the spindle mechanism. Instead of being long and pointed, the spindle was short and blunt, with a perforation entering the tip and coming out the side. Just behind this second opening was a horseshoe-shaped piece called a flyer; its two arms extended back on opposite sides of the spindle. Each arm had a row of small metal hooks. Between the two arms the spindle shaft supported a spool or bobbin, which was free to revolve on its own. There were two pulley-wheels or whorls, a larger one on the spindle shaft, a smaller one on the bobbin. Each whorl was driven by one loop of the cord from the wheel, and the different diameters caused the bobbin to revolve a little faster than the flyer.

In preparation for spinning, the hanks of tow were tied to a vertical stick called a distaff, which was supported on an arm from the base of the spinning-wheel. Another requirement was a small container of water, into which the spinner could dip her fingers. Wool was lubricated with grease, but flax had to be moistened with water. To start spinning, the operator threaded some already spun yarn through the opening in the spindle, up to one of the hooks on the flyer, and then to the bobbin, where it was secured. Now the wheel was started with a push and kept turning by rhythmic pressing on the treadle. A tuft of moistened tow was twisted onto the end of the yarn, and as the spindle whirled around, the tow was twisted into a thread, drawn through the

74 Flax heckle, menno-
nite, and heckled tow

75 Flax wheel, Quebec

76 Spinning wool yarn
on a flax wheel, Black
Creek Pioneer Village

opening in the spindle, and fed by the flyer onto the bobbin. As the bobbin revolved a little faster than the flyer, it took up any slack and produced a tight winding of the linen thread.

There were variations in the design of flax-wheels in different parts of Canada. The usual model, with the spindle mounted in a horizontal line with the wheel, was favoured by the French Canadians, and by most of the settlers from England and the United States. But the Pennsylvania Germans brought a spinning-wheel in which the spindle was mounted above the drive. A similar design, called a castle-wheel, was brought over by settlers from the Scottish Highlands.

Spinning flax was an art that demanded skill and experience. Good coordination was needed to operate the treadle and at the same time feed the two at the proper rate and tension onto the spindle. A tightly and uniformly twisted thread was the mark of an expert. Unfortunately, the complex operations involved in the preparation of flax for spinning led to the decline of the art in the 1830s, and its disappearance about 1850. This trend was accelerated by the appearance of cheap cotton in Canada following the reciprocity treaty of 1854, and the introduction of power-operated spinning mills in the 1850s. Domestic spinning of both linen and wool disappeared except as a means of producing very special fabrics.

DYEING

The natural colour of wool is white, which is not always desirable for textiles, especially those used for clothing. To get a light grey colour about one-third black wool was combined with the white in spinning. Cloth made of such yarn was called homespun, a term that has come to mean anything that is unsophisticated.

A more versatile, and more complicated, way of adding colour to textiles was the use of dyes. Dyeing was usually done at the yarn stage, although it could be applied to the woven fabric. Because imported dyes were expensive, the colonists relied mostly on colouring from wild or cultivated plants. The only commercial dye that was widely used was indigo, which was needed to produce a good blue colour. Of the local sources of dye, dandelion roots gave a reddish colour, blueberries a purplish blue, and onion skins a brownish yellow. The dye liquor was made by crushing the raw material, then steeping and boiling it in water. After straining, the liquid was diluted to the desired strength.

Before dyeing, wool had to be thoroughly washed with soap and water to remove the last trace of grease. This was not necessary with linen. The clean yarn was then immersed in the dye liquor, which was placed on the fire and allowed to simmer for an hour or more. The depth of the colouring depended on the duration of simmering and the strength of the dye. After dyeing, the yarn or fabric was rinsed until no more colour came away.

For brighter colour and more tenacious dyeing, the material was treated with a mordant. This was a chemical solution which reacted with the wool or linen and the dye to produce a more intimate union. Commonest mordants were solutions of alum (potassium aluminium sulphate) and cream of tartar (potassium tartrate). Retention of the colour, or 'fixing', was also improved by soaking the material after dyeing in a solution of tannic acid, or tartar emetic (potassium antimony tartrate).

The dyeing operation was usually done in the open or in a shed some distance from the house. The simmering dye or mordant produced unpleasant odours which made the process unpopular with those not engaged in it. Dyeing was usually done in large iron pots, although copper and brass receptacles were also used.

WEAVING

Weaving the woollen or linen yarn into cloth was done through most of colonial times on hand-looms. Although the detailed construction of these looms varied somewhat depending on the national traditions of the colonists, the basic arrangement was that of the western European loom. The frame was of heavy beams, and might be about seven feet from front to back, four feet wide, and five feet high. At the rear was a roller, called the warp beam, on which the longitudinal strands or warp were wound. Tension was maintained by means of weights on ropes. At the front was another roller, the cloth beam, on which the woven material was taken up, and which was held in position between windings by a ratchet wheel.

Between the two end reels were the harnesses, two or more in number. The harness was a lattice of vertical cords or wires called heddles, stretched between two horizontal wooden bars.

77 Dyeing wool yarn. Upper Canada Village, Morrisburg, Ontario

78 Two-harness loom

At the mid-point of each heddle was a little eyelet, through which one strand of the warp was strung. The harnesses were counter-balanced, one against the other, and were moved up and down by means of foot treadles. Pressure on one treadle pulled down its harness with that part of the warp threaded through its heddles, and because of the pulley suspension, the other harness was raised, with its part of the warp. This differential movement produced a low, triangular space between the warp strands that were up and those that were down. This space called the shed, and through it the shuttle was pushed.

Preparing the warp for threading on the loom was a special operation. It was done on a warping-frame, usually mounted on a wall. This had two rows of pegs projecting along each lateral margin. In addition, there was an extra peg near one upper corner and one lower corner. In warping, the yarn was strung back and forth from opposite pegs. Between the first peg and the extra peg each yarn strand was crossed over the preceding strand. The same was usually done between the last peg and its extra peg. After the required number of strands were strung, the 'cross' was tied with a short piece of yarn and the warp removed from the frame. The crosses kept the individual strands in proper relationship, even though the warp as a whole might be folded, or even chain-knotted. The purpose in having two crosses was to have a replacement if anything happened to release one of them.

Before putting the warp on the loom, the cross was spread out between two 'lease sticks', smooth rods longer than the width of the warp. When these sticks were tied together, the ends of the warp strands could be cut and threaded individually through the eyelets of the heddles.

The transverse strands of the weaving, called the weft, were carried in the shuttle, usually a boat-shaped piece of wood with a hollowed-out space in the middle in which a bobbin of yarn could be inserted. As the loaded shuttle was skidded from one side of the shed to the other, it left behind a transverse strand of yarn. This was pushed tight against the previous strand by a comb-like device called a batten. After each 'throw' of the shuttle and push of the batten, the opposite treadle was depressed, reversing the position of the two parts of the warp. Each weft strand was thus caught between two opposing strands of the warp, some of which went over the weft, some under. The simplest arrangement, plain weaving, was a one-to-one alternation. For this the warp strands were threaded through the harnesses alternately, the first through

harness No. 1, the second through No. 2, the third through No. 1, and so on. But other threadings were possible, such as the first strand through No. 1 and the next two or three through No. 2.

The tension to which the strands of the warp were subjected required a strong, tightly-spun yarn. Only a very good spinner could produce this in wool, and it was common practice to use linen for the warp and wool for the weft. The resultant cloth was called linsey-woolsey. Later, when cotton yarn became available, it was used instead of linen for the warp, but the name linsey-woolsey was retained for composite fabric.

Colour patterns in the cloth were produced by using different-coloured yarn in separate shuttles. More than one colour of yarn could also be used in the warp, and by combining various alternations in the colours of warp and weft, complicated patterns like those of tartans could be produced.

The possible variations in both weave and colour were enormously increased by the use of four harnesses instead of two. This provided eight different ways in which the warp strands could be threaded through the harnesses: 1,2,3,4; 4,3,2,1; 2,3,4,1; 1,4,2,3; 3,4,1,2; 2,1,4,3; 4,1,2,3; 3,2,1,4. The arrangement could be changed with each set of four strands, as long as the strands of an odd-numbered harness were followed by those of an even-numbered harness, as in the following arrangement: 1,2,3,4,3,2,1,4. Such complex threading of the warp, combined with proper manipulation of the treadles, made possible an almost infinite number of patterns. The possibilities of the four-harness loom and various coloured yarns in warp and weft were well exploited in the weaving of woollen bed covers, variously called coverlets, counterpanes, or bed-spreads, which provided decoration as well as warmth to the bed. Most of the patterns consisted of squares and rectangles of contrasting colours, and the relationships of the colours would be opposite on one side of the cloth to that on the other. If one side were predominantly dark and the other predominantly light, the pattern was called 'summer and winter'.

Threading the warp so that a strand from an odd-numbered harness was followed by one from an even-numbered harness permitted the weaver to do plain over-and-under weaving, no matter how complicated the warping might otherwise be. This possibility was exploited in the type of weaving called overshot, commonly used for coverlets. Two shuttles were used, one for the ground colour, usually white, the other for a heavier, coloured yarn. The warping was set up for the particular pattern to be followed. The weaver first depressed harnesses 1 and 3, or 2 and 4. This formed a simple shed of alternating strands, through which the shuttle with the ground-colour yarn was thrown. This was called the tabby weave. Then the treadles were depressed in accordance with the pattern, and the shuttle with the coloured yarn was thrown. Two, three, or even twelve strands of the warp might be 'overshot' by the coloured weft. In overshot weaving, as in other techniques, the weaver followed a diagram on ruled paper, a little like a musical score.

Width of the cloth that could be woven was limited by the distance that the weaver could throw the shuttle through the shed. In practice this was about 30 inches. Blankets and coverlets were woven in two strips, which were sewn together to provide the required width. But the invention of the flying shuttle made it possible to weave in widths much exceeding 30 inches. The loom was provided on each side of the shed space with a little paddle hung from a short track. A cord was attached to the paddle, and a quick jerk on the cord sent the shuttle flying through the shed to the opposite side, where the other paddle was ready to propel it back again. Because of the impact of shuttle on paddle, the tips of the flying shuttle were shod with metal points.

Unlike spinning, which was considered to be women's work, suitable for the home, weaving was usually done by men, and in a special location. Looms were too big for the usual home, and the operation of weaving, with repeating pushing of treadles and throwing of shuttle, was considered too strenuous to be expected of women. Except in the larger communities, weaving was usually done by itinerant weavers, who set up their looms for a time and wove the locally spun yarn to meet the local demand before moving on to another location.

Even the four-harness loom could produce only patterns with simple geometrical designs. This limitation was overcome by the Jacquard loom, which was invented in France in 1801, but which did not become prominent in North America until the 1840s. The Jacquard loom had, in effect, a separate harness for each strand of the warp. The raising of any particular strand was governed by a punched card, which was wrapped around a cylinder with rows of holes. As the cylinder was revolved, the holes that were exposed by the perforations of the card tripped a device which raised the corresponding heddle wire, while the holes that were covered by imperforated card allowed their particular heddle wire to remain down. So the perforations of the card could be 'programmed' for a pattern limited only by the number of strands in the warp. After one revolution of the cylinder the card was replaced by the next one in the series, and so, instead of a geometrical pattern, an elaborate or pictorial design could be produced. In the 1840s and 1850s, Jacquard weaving was widespread in the United States, and the designs often incorporated American patriotic motifs, such as the eagle and the flag. The American Civil War (1861–65) disrupted the Jacquard-weaving industry, and many of the looms were brought to Canada, and operated for some years by local weavers. Many of the American patterns were retained, and appeared in Canadian homes even while there was a strong anti-American sentiment because of political and military events.

Just as spinning machinery, operated by water or steam power, superseded the hand-operated spinning wheels, so power looms took the place of hand looms in the 1850s and 1860s. These could have very wide sheds and almost any number of harnesses. The shuttle was propelled through the shed at high velocity, and the whole operation proceeded rapidly. This equipment, set up in 'woollen mills', took over the weaving of regular cloth, but the hand loom in various forms remained in use for some years longer as a means of weaving coverlets and draperies.

A widely used type of bed cover in French Canada was the catalogne. Originally the name was applied to white woollen or linen blankets made in Spain or southern France. In New France they were used until they became badly worn. In order to rejuvenate them, they were cut into narrow strips, which were woven as the weft into a warp of wool or cotton. The resultant fabric was heavy, almost rug-like, but with excellent insulating qualities.

RUGS

Floor coverings of various sorts were woven by the colonists. A simple type was plain-woven, using various coloured yarns in the warp. Loom-widths of this were sewn together to produce the required area of floor covering. As the colours were in longitudinal bands, there was no problem of matching patterns between strips. True rugs were made by pulling or pushing little loops of yarn through a coarsely woven cotton or hemp base. A wide variety of colours could be used, and the French Canadian hooked rug became well known as a deoration as well as a warm floor covering. Rugs were also made using strips of discarded fabric instead of yarn, or the strips might be braided and sewn together spirally, to make a circular or oval rug.

KNITTING

Knitting is a kind of weaving using a single strand of yarn and two skewer-like needles. The yarn is 'cast' over one needle in a series of loops. Using the other needle, each loop is picked off and another loop pushed through it, forming a second row of loops. This operation, repeated back and forth from one needle to the other, creates a strip of fabric the width of which is governed by the length of the needles, and the weight by the coarseness of the yarn and the diameter of the needles. Knitted fabric is much more elastic than loom-woven cloth, and was always favoured for undergarments. Even after the mechanical knitting machine came into use early in the nineteenth century, the Canadian housewife continued to knit quantities of stockings, gloves, mittens, and scarves for her family. Knitting was practised not only for its useful products, but also because it permitted women to enjoy a little well-earned leisure without feeling guilty of idleness.

QUILTING

The device of sewing a layer of unwoven fibres, such as cotton or wool, between two layers of fabric originated in eastern countries and spread to Europe during the Middle Ages. In the Orient it was used for making clothes, but in North America it was adapted to the making of bed covers, called quilts. One reason for the popularity of quilt-making was that scraps of material left over from other sewing projects could be used. These pieces were sewn to the base fabric, usually a cotton sheet, with a layer of unwoven cotton 'batting' between. Using a previously laid-out design, the various pieces were arranged in patterns, many of which were traditional to different regions and cultural groups. For example, the 'log-cabin' pattern was made up of alternating squares, each consisting of parallel strips of various colours. Patterns with an hexagonal arrangement were called 'honey-comb'. Various forms of the eight-sided star, and the quarter-circle 'fan', were other popular motifs. Some patterns were extremely intricate, a *tour de force* of the skilful seamstress. In contrast, some quilts were made with no apparent attempt to create a pattern; these were called crazy quilts.

In addition to the various patterns made possible by using patches of different colours, the ornamentation of the quilts could be increased with elaborate stitches of bright coloured threads. During the nineteenth century a different method of quilting became popular; this was called tufting. The material used was candlewick, a loosely spun cotton yarn. Loops of this were sewn through the quilt at points along a predesigned pattern. The loops were then tied and cut, leaving the ends to form tufts. Unless combined with conventional quilting, tufting could only be used with a wool filling, as it would not keep cotton batting from shifting during handling or washing.

Quilting was done with the base fabric stretched on a large, rectangular wooden frame, which could be dismantled when not in use. For one person to make a quilt would take a long time, during which the frame could not be put away. Sometimes the problem was solved by hoisting the frame to the ceiling on pulleys. The usual procedure, however, was to have a quilting party, a kind of 'bee' for the women. With workers on the sides of the frame the quilting proceeded rapidly. Work was accompanied by animated conversation, and was followed by refreshments. The quality of the needlework must have varied with the experience of the various workers, but skill at quilting, like spinning, was an ability much admired in women.

EMBROIDERY

The decoration of fabrics by sewing into them stitches of coloured yarn is the art of embroidery. In oriental countries it was carried to fantastic elaboration. In colonial North America, embroidery was used mainly to make small decorative pieces, such as table centres, seat covers, and handkerchiefs. The base was of cotton or linen, and the embroidery yarn was usually of coloured wool.

Embroidery was taught to girls at an early stage in their domestic training, and skill in it was another accomplishment that was highly esteemed. As a demonstration of skill and an exercise in the art, young girls embroidered a rectangular piece of cotton or linen with the letters of the alphabet, Biblical quotations, or mottoes with elevating sentiments. There was an elaborate decorative outer border, and spaces filled with stars, anchors, animal figures, or abstract designs. Also included was the name and age of the seamstress, and the date of completion of the work. These productions were known as samplers, from the word exemplar, and they provided a reference of the various stitches for future work. They also had some of the status of graduation diplomas. Framed and hung on the wall, they were proof of proficiency in the art, and for future generations they were heirlooms, a record of people and their ideals.

About the middle of the nineteenth century, methods of mechanical embroidery were introduced, and the art became an object of commerce, or at best the routine following of a set pattern. One form that enjoyed a 'mid-Victorian' popularity was known as Berlin work. In this, a piece of coarse fabric was used, on which had already been embroidered by machine a decorative design, with the background areas of the fabric open. Ladies filled this in with coloured yarn of their choice by sewing the interstices of the weave, as in darning. The product was tapestry-like and of good wearing strength, and was commonly used to cover the seats of chairs. The name came from the fact that many of the designs used were from patterns produced in Berlin, Prussia. The modern techniques of gros-point and petit-point are similar.

VERY CHILDISH
I MUST ADMIT.

Don't listen to them.
They don't know what
they're talking about.

10
Clothing

The clothing worn by the people of colonial Canada was basically
that of the European country from which they came. French
peasants brought with them the simple working clothes of their
province, while administrators and soldiers retained the elaborate
costumes or uniforms of their class. During the British colonial
régime, French Canada was cut off from France, and the habitant
developed styles and accessories of his own. Meanwhile the influx
of the Loyalists brought English costumes to Canada, and this
trend was greatly reinforced by the waves of British immigration
in the nineteenth century.

The influence of European styles on colonial clothing was
modified in several ways. First, the colonists were separated from
the sources of fashion by 3,000 miles of ocean. Replacement of
clothing was expensive and slow, and styles were retained in
America long after they had lost their popularity at home. Clothes
were mended and remodelled many more times than if their source
of replacement had been close at hand. Sturdy or expensive items
were passed on as legacies.

A second important factor was the influence of local conditions.
Winters were long and cold in the new land, and spring brought
a sea of mud. Summers were hot and sultry, and spawned hordes
of stinging insects. To meet such conditions, European dress was
modified, made warmer for winter, looser and cooler for summer.
Footwear had to be suitable for snow or mud. In part, the adaptation consisted of borrowing from the clothing of the native
people, either by direct use, or by incorporating the ideas as
modifications of European dress.

A third factor was the scarcity of cloth from which to make new
clothing. The fine textiles of Europe were expensive in Canada,
and not always suitable for local conditions. Cotton and silk could

not be produced in Canada, and the facilities for weaving wool and linen were for many years very limited. The textiles that were produced were mostly of coarse weave and simple colour.

Another local effect was the levelling of style between the different classes of society. In seventeenth- and eighteenth-century France, and even in nineteenth-century Britain, there was a very great difference between what the gentry wore and what was the dress of the farmer and labourer. In the New World the upper classes tried to retain this distinction of dress, but replacements were hard to get, style changes could not be followed closely, and the way of life of even the upper classes involved outdoor activities and even manual labour. Finery had to be reserved for socially important occasions.

FRENCH CANADA
In 1608, when the first permanent settlement was established, European dress was just emerging from the renaissance styles that characterized Tudor England and France of the Medicis. Short, slashed trunks and thigh-length hose were being replaced by breeches that fell below the knees and stockings that were only long enough to overlap. Tight-fitting doublet and narrow sleeves were disappearing in favour of loose, square-cut jacket with ample sleeves. The circular, projecting, pleated ruff was being replaced by a gracefully falling lace or linen collar. Beret-like caps, with little or no brim were losing out to voluminous felt hats with high crowns and wide, flexible brims.

There are no contemporary portraits of Samuel de Champlain, but later artists, with reason, have shown him wearing a moderately tight doublet with wide sleeves, voluminous breeches, high leather boots, and a wide-brimmed, plumed hat. Some have added a broad, square-cut jerkin, but it is more probable that his outer garment was a short cape. The soldiers and sailors who accompanied Champlain wore much the same clothing, but of simple cut with little ornamentation.

Men's undergarments of this period consisted of shirts with long sleeves worn under the jackets, and cotton drawers inside the breeches. Stockings were either of knitted wool or of sewn wool or cotton. They were held up with garters, in contrast to the earlier full-length hose, which had to be hooked to the trunks.

The French were not long on the shores of the St Lawrence before they began adopting or adapting articles of Indian clothing to their own use. The first to be taken over was probably footwear. When the high leather boots of France wore out there were few cobblers to replace them, and the leather moccasin would be the natural substitute. These were the high-topped variety, with leather lacings up the leg. Leather jackets took the place of woollen coats, and fur caps displaced felt hats. For winter wear, the native furs were used to make warm jackets and cloaks.

The changing styles in European dress during the seventeenth century, under the influence of Louis xiv, were reflected with a time lag in New France. Both male and female costumes became more elaborate than in almost any time in history. Breeches were voluminous. Waistcoasts reached well below the waist, and coats were even longer. Sleeves were short, with exaggerated cuffs, below which the lace of the shirt sleeve extended. Neckwear was a linen scarf, tied in a formal bow, or twisted with simulated carelessness (the Steinkirk). The crown of the hat became lower, and was decorated with ribbons as well as feathers. Wigs of various styles, but always curled, were worn by gentlemen in public. Shoes were moderately high-heeled, with prominent tongues. But men usually wore boots, even indoors. These had a wide upper part, which was folded down to form a flaring rim. Cloaks were still worn as an outer garment for warmth, but later on a true overcoat made its appearance.

During the eighteenth century, changes in European costumes were gradual. The grotesque male dress of the Louis xiv period gave way to more functional styles, although still elaborate by later standards. Long, buttoned, sleeveless waistcoats were worn over linen shirts with ruffled sleeves. Breeches were tight-fitting, and overlapped the stockings just below the knees. Over all was a long coat, with expanded cuffs, from which the ruffled shirt-sleeves projected. The linen or silk scarf remained as neckwear, wound around the neck and allowed to fall in front.

Wigs continued to be worn throughout the eighteenth century, but varied greatly in size and style with different classes of society and different years. Hats for most of the century were the tricorne, made by fastening the wide, flexible brim to the crown in three places. It was ornamented with feathers or buckles. The heavy leather boots, which had been worn almost everywhere by men in the seventeenth century, became restricted to outdoor use, especially riding, and assumed a neater, more close-fitting style. Men's shoes were similar to those of the seventeenth century.

Not many women came to New France in the days of Champlain, but those who did included ladies of quality, such as Hélène de

Champlain, wife of the Governor, and Jeanne Mance, founder of the Hôtel Dieu in Montreal. At that time the fashionable women's dress in France consisted of a voluminous skirt and underskirt, a tight-fitting bodice with wide sleeves, and an elaborate lace neckpiece, either projecting as ruffles or falling gracefully on the shoulders. Such a costume was unsuited for the pioneer conditions of New France, and we can assume that the skirts and sleeves became less voluminous and the bodices less confining. The neckpiece was probably replaced by a simply draped scarf. Aprons would be worn for household duties.

On going out in cold weather, seventeenth-century ladies wore a cloak with a hood. A fur muff for the hands was more for warmth than for fashion. The ordinary shoes for ladies, low with moderate heels, were quite unsuited to the Canadian winter or spring, and must have been replaced for outdoor use by wooden shoes (sabots) or leather boots.

Women's fashions were extravagant in the middle and late seventeenth century, but in comparison to the elaboration of men's costumes, the changes were moderate. The wide pleated skirt maintained its popularity, sometimes enhanced by a partial overskirt, sometimes open in front to show a colourful petticoat. Bodices became even tighter and longer than before. Jeanne Mance, one of the better-dressed women of the French colony, left a wardrobe on her death in 1673 which included 33 hats or caps, 30 blouses, 5 jackets, 7 skirts, 1 gown, 5 pairs of stockings, and 3 pairs of shoes.

The exaggerated female costumes of the eighteenth century were probably not seen very often in New France. It is said that Madame de Vaudreuil, wife of the last French governor, tried to create a miniature Versailles at Quebec, but military events, alas, brought this epoch to a close. Skirts that projected widely at the sides, supported by an elaborate metal framework called a panier, would have been incongruous in an environment in which even ladies of quality had to meet the challenge of snow, mud, freezing wind, or blistering sun. So too with the preposterous coiffures, like architectural monstrosities.

To the habitant, the elaborate and changing fashions of Europe meant little. In the early years his basic attire consisted of woollen drawers, a pair of breeches reaching well below the knees, a woollen or linen shirt, long woollen stockings, and leather boots. A jacket of heavy wool or of leather kept out the rain and wind. For those who spent much time in the forest, such as the *couriers du bois*, leather was the principal material of clothing, as it was for the native people, but the Frenchmen cut and sewed it in the manner of cloth garments, making jackets, breeches, and short leggings, instead of the Indian breech-clout, long leggings, and pull-over shirt.

During the eighteenth century, while the urban French Canadians, and after 1760 the English upper classes, endeavoured to follow the fashions of Europe, the habitant was evolving his own style of dress, which was traditional by the early part of the nineteenth century. A woollen jacket, called a capote, was worn over a coloured shirt. Breeches were loose, with the lower ends tucked into heavy woollen stockings. A distinctive woollen cap (toque), conical in shape and loose enough to be pulled down over the ears, was worn most of the year, but was replaced in summer by a felt or straw hat. Shoes of moccasin type were widely worn, but heavy leather boots were also available.

Freedom from even the second-hand dictates of fashion allowed the habitant to develop his own ideas of ornamentation of dress. Bright colours were used for capote and toque. Epaulets and cuffs were added in imitation of military dress. Most conspicuous were the brightly-coloured sashes, finger-woven in the distinctive arrow pattern (*ceinture fléche*). Miniature versions of these sashes were worn as ornamental garters.

Women's costumes among the eighteenth- and early nineteenth-century habitants were less distinctive than the men's, but they also used bright colours. The full skirt and the apron were characteristic. Jackets were simple, with moderately tight sleeves. Some sort of shawl or scarf was draped around the neck and shoulders. The cloth cap persisted into the nineteenth century, but was eventually replaced by the bonnet.

ENGLISH CANADA

The coming of the Loyalist settlers to the remaining British colonies after the Revolution brought the manners of dress that had developed in the American colonies. Styles and colours were restrained, under the influence of Puritan and Quaker traditions. But the clothes worn by the Loyalist immigrants and those of the middle-class French Canadians were essentially the same. It was only with the habitant dress that there was a striking contrast. A distinctive working-man's costume for English Canada was yet to come.

The French Revolution brought about a change in fashions for both men and women that had a profound effect throughout Europe and America. The revolutionists associated the elaborate fashions of the French aristocracy with the despotism of the monarchy. First to go were the knee-length breeches (culottes), and the ardent revolutionist was known as 'sans-culotte'. They were replaced by trousers, derived from the long loose breeches of the French peasant. Fashion at first favoured a tight version, not too different in outline from the knee breeches. Later they became loose, with a loop to go under the arch of the shoe. These garments were also called pantaloons, after a comic character in the Italian theatre, who traditionally wore them well before they were accepted by fashion.

Lengthening the breeches into trousers was accompanied by shortening the waistcoat into something more like the modern 'vest'. Also the long, flowing coat was cut away in the front, leaving a remnant behind and creating the tail coat. The neck-piece or cravat, instead of being wound directly around the neck, was looped and tied around the collar, a starched extension of the shirt. It could be of a contrasting colour to the coat, but more often was black. This was the beginning of the necktie. In men's hats the brim became narrower and the crown higher, eventually producing the top hat, which in one form or another was the characteristic male headgear of the nineteenth century.

Women's costumes were even more drastically affected by the revolution than were men's, but curiously underwent a subsequent reaction towards the elaboration of the eighteenth century. The leaders of republican France were impressed by the traditions of ancient Greece and Rome, as they understood them, and this was reflected in the 'classic' style of dress. The waist was set very high, and from it the skirt hung down in long, slender lines. What bodice was left was not confining, but the sleeves were rather tight. Shawls or kerchiefs were worn around the neck and shoulders. Elaborate hair styles were abandoned, and short hair permitted the use of neat, close-fitting bonnets. Ladies shoes were low, almost heelless, and more like slippers.

Less than twenty years after this revolution in women's costume, skirts were beginning to expand again, at first by the use of heavy petticoats. Later they were reinforced with woven horsehair, and in the 1850s by an elaborate framework of wire hoops held together with tapes. In this way was created the hoop-skirt, usually called the crinoline, which by the 1860s had changed the female silhouette into that of an enormous bell. Accompanying this

80 *Lady Swells*, from a painting by James Duncan (1806–1882). Winter costume in Quebec, *c.* 1860

ballooning of the skirt was a narrowing and tightening of the bodice, with increased dependence on the whalebone corset. Sleeves became voluminous, at first above the elbows, but later for the whole length. The bonnet, which originally enclosed the sides as well as the top of the head, became smaller and eventually took the form of a dainty hat of silk or straw, perched on the top of the head and held in place with ribbons tied under the chin. Military headgear was the inspiration for the pillbox and the Empress Eugenie hats that were popular in the 1860s.

The clothing of farmers and labourers in English Canada was neither as distinctive nor as picturesque as it was among the habitants. Differences from fashionable clothing were in the plainer, sturdier materials and the looser cut. Trousers were adopted early because of their utility, and were usually tucked into high-topped leather boots. As cotton fabrics became generally available they were used for shirts and for smock-like jackets. Overcoats had short shoulder capes that helped to keep out the rain. Felt or straw hats with wide brims and rounded crowns were worn at work, but military-style caps were also common.

The housewife's costume retained the full skirt but without padding. The blouse was only moderately tight, and there was the inevitable apron. Crinolines and other extravagances, if worn at all, were only for special occasions. Shawls were worn outdoors, but for cold weather the cloak with hood was comfortable with the full skirt.

Restraint in dress was carried to extremes among the Mennonites and Quakers of Upper Canada, who used plain, dark cloth cut in simple lines, without any ornamentation. Even buttons were too ostentatious for some sects, and clothes were secured with concealed wire fasteners. To find picturesque clothing outside of French Canada, one had to go to the far west. In the Red River Settlement, both the French Métis and the Scottish farmers adopted leather garments, for cloth was scarce, while deer and buffalo skins were readily available. Leather trousers and jackets were combined with woollen shirts and socks. Headgear, if any, was a cloth hat or cap from the trading post.

The goldfields of British Columbia brought miners from the western United States, who wore their characteristic costume of loose shirt and trousers, high leather boots, and wide-brimmed hats. Only the holstered pistol was needed to complete the 'wild-west' costume, but British authorities did not encourage the carrying of hand guns.

MAKING CLOTHES

Hats and overcoats were obtained by purchase or barter from the local merchant, but other articles of clothing were made as required. The cloth itself might be the produce of a local loom, but when power-driven weaving mills became common, the commercially manufactured textiles were more likely to be used. Few housewives were competent to cut out the pieces for a dress or suit, and this task was usually given to an experienced dressmaker or seamstress. But all the female members of the family could participate in the sewing. The visit of the dressmaker was a family event, and might happen only once a year. But worn-out clothes were taken apart and the pieces used as patterns for new garments. With the advent of fashion magazines, such as *Godey's Lady's Book* in the 1840s, fashionable and sophisticated patterns became available, not only to the professional dressmaker, but also to the housewife with an average skill as a seamstress.

Men's clothing was usually cut and sewn by a tailor, who could take the proper measurements. The cloth, however, might be provided by the customer. Some communities, such as the Pennsylvania Germans of Upper Canada and the Highland Scottish of Nova Scotia, made men's coats and trousers from the locally woven wool (homespun). Shirts and underwear were commonly made at home, and socks were knitted by the housewife or her daughter. Shoes were usually obtained from the professional cobbler, who might have a shop, or who might travel from house to house, providing footwear for the whole family in one visit. Even the shoemaker's craft, however, was sometimes practised by the head of the family. The product might not be stylish, nor the fit very comfortable. But even the shoes produced by the professional did not conform closely to the individual foot shape, or even differentiate between right and left; these conformities could be produced by wear.

Children's clothing was usually the altered 'hand-me-downs' of their parents or older brothers and sisters. New dresses and suits, if they had to be provided, were miniatures of adult clothing. By the middle of the nineteenth century, interest in styles extended to children's clothing, and special designs became popular. Girls' skirts were short, revealing long stockings or lace pantalettes. Boys wore knee breeches, a curious reversion to eighteenth-century style, and short jackets, fastened with a single button at the collar. Little boys wore dresses until about six years of age.

Men's silk or felt hats had to be made by the professional hatter, but straw hats could be made at home. This was done by soaking straw in water, then braiding it into a kind of rope. While this was still wet it was run through a press consisting of two small wooden rollers. This changed the rope shape to a ribbon shape. The flat bands of straw were then coiled and sewn together over a suitably shaped form.

LAUNDRY

Until the middle 1800s, western European methods of washing clothes and bedding had remained unchanged for centuries. The essential aid was soap, which for good results should be free from excess alkali. Unfortunately, this was seldom true of the home-made soap of colonial times, and what with this and the excess use of boiling water, it seems likely that clothes wore out more quickly in the wash-tub than on the wearer.

The principle of laundering with soap is that the soap emulsifies the grease in the soiled cloth, and this emulsion with its contained dirt is removed by manipulation and rinsing. In a well-managed colonial household the preparation for each wash day began the night before. Coloured garments were separated to avoid 'running' of the dyes. Then the clothes were put to soak overnight in cold water. The actual washing was done in tepid water, the soap being rubbed into the cloth, which was then repeatedly squeezed, rubbed against itself, and wrung out. This operation was repeated in another tub-full of warm water. To remove all of the soap, the clothes were doused and wrung out in clean water until no further suds emerged.

Woollen fabrics presented a special problem because of their tendency to shrink when washed, which was produced by the twisting of the fibres. Shrinkage could be minimized by using 'soft' water (rain water or melted snow), a good quality soap, and by squeezing and pressing but not rubbing or wringing. The amount of soap required could be reduced by adding ox gall, a natural detergent, which was extracted from the gall bladder of an ox.

The proper techniques of washing clothes were seldom followed in the colonial home. Usually the clothes were simply dumped into a pot or tank of soapy water and then boiled on the open fire or the stove. To remove the clothes from the scalding water, wooden tongs were used. The inevitable shrinkage to woollens that resulted from boiling was partly corrected by pulling and stretching during the drying process.

By the use of a wash-board a little of the drudgery was taken out of washing by hand. This was a board about two feet long, on one side of which numerous transverse grooves were carved. It was placed inside the tub with the clothes, leaning against the rim, and the well-soaped garments were rubbed up and down vigorously across the corrugations.

Mechanical washing machines developed by stages during the nineteenth century. An early device was a conical wooden or tin plunger on a handle. By working this up and down vigorously in the tub of soapy clothes, adequate manipulation could be obtained without direct contact with the hands. Then there was a roller device consisting of two corrugated wooden cylinders mounted to rotate against each other when turned with a crank. By repeatedly passing the soaped clothes through this rotary press, the effect was obtained of scrubbing on a flat wash board.

The first true washing machine was a rectangular wooden tub pivoted at the mid-length so that it could be rocked end-to-end by means of a handle. This rocking caused the soap solution to circulate through the clothes, reacting with the grease and carrying away the dirt. In the rotary washing machine a dash-wheel shaped like a stool with legs was oscillated one way and the other by means of a gear mechanism and a crank.

There still remained the tiresome task of rinsing and wringing. A roller device similar to the washer but with smooth cylinders made this stage a little easier by pressing out the water as the clothes were wound through. After as much as possible of the water had been squeezed out, the clothes were hung on a line or rack to dry in the sun and wind. Freezing of the damp clothes in winter created no problem, and even helped to bleach white fabrics.

The dried clothes still had to be smoothed of folds and wrinkles. In some German communities this was done with a smoothing board, a corrugated tool shaped a little like a cricket bat. In use it was drawn repeatedly over the spread-out garment. But in most parts of Canada the smoothing was done by 'ironing', that is, by moving a hot iron weight over the clothes. These weights or irons were usually triangular blocks with a horizontal handle on top. Heating them directly in the fireplace would have made them dirty, so they were made hollow; into the cavity a heated block of cast iron or brick was introduced before using. There were also large irons like miniature stoves, in which a charcoal fire could be lit. When kitchen stoves came into use, solid irons which could be placed directly on the stove top replaced the hollow versions. The 'sad-irons' had the handle cast in one piece with the body and when hot had to be manipulated with a heavy cloth for insulation. Ironing was done on a board, usually tapered at one end, and padded with layers of flannel and cotton.

In addition to the various kinds of 'flat-iron', there were special irons for particular purposes. The fluted finish of shirt fronts and cuffs was obtained by pressing between two corrugated iron plates, one flat, the other rocker-shaped. There was also a fluting machine, involving two small corrugated metal rollers turned by

81 Wash board and wooden wash tub

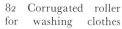

82 Corrugated roller for washing clothes

83   Goffering   iron.
Erindale, Ontario

a handle. The rollers were heated by introducing hot iron rods into the hollow centres. Then there was the goffering iron, a finger-shaped metal tube mounted on a stand. A heated iron was placed inside, and the collars and cuffs of shirts were drawn across the outer surface, back and forth, to produce a smooth finish.

Ironing was easier if the clothes were slightly damp. They were either sprinkled with water just before applying the hot iron, or they were 'dampened down' under a wet cloth overnight. To obtain a stiff, shiny finish, garments such as shirts and aprons were 'starched' before ironing. This involved soaking them in a watery suspension of starch. They were then partially dried indoors, and ironed while still slightly damp. Starching not only improved the appearance of the garment but also increased resistance to soiling.

In spite of mechanical aids, the washing and ironing of clothes and bedding were drudgery, the least pleasurable of all household activities. Not only was the actual work fatiguing, but working over tubs of near-boiling water or beside a hot stove was unpleasant even in winter and intolerable in summer. Sometimes there were serious injuries caused by the spilling of scalding water. In the more prosperous homes there was a separate room for the laundry, and servants to do the heavy work. But usually it was the housewife herself who did the washing, in the kitchen. The only help from husband or son was the bringing in of water from the well, and the carrying out of the used wash-water.

11

Work in the Forests

Except for the prairies, on the edge of which the Red River Settlement established its precarious foothold in 1813, all parts of the future Canada that were settled in colonial times were densely forested. In the more southerly areas the predominant trees were the deciduous hardwoods, such as white oak, maple, birch, walnut, beech, and hickory. The density and heaviness of forest growth are hard to believe from modern experience. Oak trees six feet or more in diameter are on record. Even such lesser trees as birch and cherry achieved what would be called a giant size today.

The sad fate of this wealth of timber was to be destroyed in the process of land clearing. Contemporary observers bemoaned this colossal waste, but what else was the would-be farmer to do? At first there was no market at all for these fine woods, and even when saw-mills were established, the amount of lumber that they could sell was far less than the available logs could have furnished if the cutters could have brought them to the mill. So if fields were to be cleared and crops sown, the only course was to destroy the forest barrier as quickly as possible.

Farther north, beyond good agricultural land, the sandy valleys between rocky ridges held primeval stands of white pine and other conifers. These were the basis of the lumbering industry, which contributed much to the economic development of the British American colonies. On the Pacific coast, stands of the giant Douglas fir were an analogous resource. Because settlement was slow in penetrating these forest areas, and because when it came it was limited to the relatively small arable parts, most of the virgin timber was still there when organized lumbering was ready to move in and reap the harvest.

FELLING THE TREES

The basic tool of the lumberman was the same axe as was used by the settler in clearing his land. It had changed little since developed in the American colonies and brought to Canada by the Loyalists. The moderately wide but thin head, the narrow, rectangular hammer surface opposite the blade, and the slightly S-curved handle with its expanded end, are the same today as they were in colonial times. The professional woodsman kept the blade honed to a razor edge, and treated his axe like the fine craftsman's tool that it was.

The felling of trees by chopping two notches, one on each side of the trunk, has been described in Chapter 2. In late colonial times the second notch was replaced by a saw cut. This was made with a 'cross-cut' saw, a long, flexible blade with deep teeth, and a handle at each end. With a man on each handle, on opposite sides of the tree, a cut was sawn opposite and a little above the already-chopped notch. With a large tree the weight of the trunk would bind the saw blade before it had penetrated far, so iron wedges were driven into the saw cut behind the blade to keep the upper and lower surfaces of wood apart.

Once on the ground, the trunk was cleared of branches, and the upper part, too narrow for lumber, was cut off. Logging was usually done in the winter, when there was abundant snow, and the logs could be hauled away by sled. The sled was a short device, intended to support one end of the log. First the log to be moved was skidded or rolled so that one end projected over another log. The sled was then pushed under this projecting end and the log secured to it with a chain. The log could then be dragged along a previously cleared and possibly iced timber road. For many years oxen provided the motive power, but later they were replaced by horses, which worked faster but required more skill in handling. If there was a steep hill on the road, this might be sanded to slow the descent, or a heavy chain could be wound around the rear end of the log to dig in and act as a brake. The destination was the bank of a lake or stream, where the log was freed from the sled and rolled down the slope onto the ice, to await the spring melting.

In manipulating logs the early woodsman had only simple tools. Poles were used as levers, and heavy spikes to separate logs. On the ice or in the water the tool was the pike, a pole 12 or 15 feet long, with a pointed and hooked end, like a seaman's gaff. In the late 1850s a new tool appeared, the invention of Joseph

Peavey of Maine, and so known forever as the peavey. It consisted of a short, stout pole, about five feet long, the lower end of which was enclosed in an iron sheath from which a sharp spike projected. From the upper end of the sheath a stout iron hook was pivoted. The user swung this hook under a log to be rolled, and with the point embedded in the wood, pushed or lifted on the handle. The leverage so obtained was sufficient to roll even a very heavy log. The peavey was modified by adding stout teeth to the inner side of the sheath, creating the cant-hook, which was very effective on land, but which did not replace the peavey in the water, as it was not as easy to free from a floating log.

THE TIMBER DRIVE

Most of the timber cut in the areas north of Lake Ontario and floated down the streams draining into that lake were 'driven' as free logs during the spring run-off. The same was true of the extensive lumbering in New Brunswick, mostly in the valley of the Saint John River. The lumbermen followed the main run of logs, trying to forestall an entanglement which could form a 'jam'. This could be freed by extricating the one or more logs that were the 'key' to the accumulation. Once these were loosened the other logs would let go with a rush, and the lumbermen would have to leap for safety. The elaborately spiked or 'caulked' lumberman's boots came later; in the early days only a few homemade spikes in the soles helped to prevent a fatal slip. Running logs was an exciting and dangerous task, calling for experience, strength, and agility. The loss of life was relatively high for a civilian occupation in those days.

In the colony of British Columbia there was seldom enough snow and ice to provide a runway for dragging logs. When they had to be hauled any distance, a pair of large wheels on a stout axle took the place of the sled. This contraption, with its trailing log, was pulled by one or two teams of horses. In the precipitous coastal country it was usually not too far to a steep slope down which the logs could be rolled to water, or slid down a wooden flume into which a stream had been diverted. Often the logs went directly into a sea inlet, where they were confined by a flexible boom made by chaining a number of logs together, end to end.

The great Douglas fir trunks, often 200 feet high and six feet in diameter at the base, would fall with a fearful crash. To avoid damage and deflection in falling, the trunks were cleared of branches while still standing. This meant that a specially skilled and daring woodsman had to ascend the tree, using climbing irons and a belt, and chop away the limbs as he went up. At a point 100 feet or more from the ground the trunk would reach a width too narrow to be usefully sawn up for lumber. Here the climber had to chop off the unwanted upper part, because in the fall of the tree it might split the valuable part of the trunk. To cut free this upper part without being dislodged by its fall, and to retain his grip while the trunk twanged like a string, the 'topper' required all his strength and experience. No wonder that he was the highest paid man in the timber crew.

THE SQUARED-TIMBER TRADE

During the French régime in Canada there was no true lumber industry. Timber was cut for building and for ship construction, but little if any was sent to Europe. Even after British rule was established, Canadian timber could not compete in the European market with that from the much closer Baltic forests. But the embargo set up by Napoleon in 1806 against exports to Britain made it necessary to turn to North America for timber, especially for the construction of naval vessels. At first this timber was obtained from the St Lawrence Valley and the lower part of the Ottawa Valley. In 1806 an event occurred that made the trade in squared timber one of the major industries of colonial Canada, and which persisted into the twentieth century.

In 1800 an American named Philemon Wright brought a party of settlers to the north shore of the Ottawa River and established them at a site just below the formidable Chaudière Falls. The settlement of Wrightville, the future city of Hull, Quebec, was intended to be a farming and trading community, but lumbering was found to be a profitable side-line. In 1806 Wright explored the timber stands along the Ottawa, upstream from Wrightville, and examined the various rapids as to the possibility of bringing down timber in the form of rafts. He tried this successfully the following year. At the Chaudière he took his rafts apart to send the logs through individually, and reassembled them below. From here it was relatively easy to float them down to the junction with the St Lawrence and thence to Quebec City, where the timbers were sold at a profit to British buyers.

From this beginning the cutting, squaring, and rafting of timber on the Ottawa became big business. The Wright family were the kings of this trade, but were soon joined by other operators with bases farther up the valley, such as Arnprior and

Pembroke. The industry demanded abundant supplies and labour. This brought in settlers long before they could have hoped for some other market for their produce. Not only did these backwoods farmers have a ready sale for their flour, vegetables, and hay, but in the winter after harvest they could 'hire out' to the lumber company with their teams of oxen or horses.

So great was the demand for supplies by the lumber camps that even the farmers could not meet it, and the lumber companies developed farms of their own around their field headquarters. So the 'station' was developed, to become a centre for the lumbering community.

SQUARING TIMBER

The logs were chopped to a square cross-section because that was the way that the British buyers wanted them. Also it made it easier to assemble the logs into rafts. But it was very wasteful of wood. A diameter of less than 12 inches was unsuitable for squaring, so the trunk above that level was cut off and left to rot. The remainder of the trunk, cut into 40 or 50 foot lengths, was chopped square, with the result that the four curved sides, which might have provided good boards, were destroyed.

Squaring timber was a complicated operation requiring special tools and skills. The 'liner', who supervised, scraped off the bark along the intended line of the cutting. This was marked more precisely by means of a chalked cord, the ends of which were held tight at the opposite ends of the log. Pulling it from the middle, the liner 'twanged' it against the wood, making a perfectly straight white line. This operation was repeated on the opposite side of the log. Axemen called scorers then notched the sides of the log vertically outside this line at intervals of about four feet, and then chopped out the intervening slabs. The final task was done by the 'hewer', who used a broad-headed axe, one side of which was flat, the other slightly concave. As most hewers were right-handed, the axe handle was inserted so that the flat side of the head was on the left or log side of the axe. The hewer worked his way down the side of the log, slicing off neatly the remaining wood to the chalk line. Only a skilled axeman could keep the face truly vertical. After finishing one side of the log, he worked back along the other. If a left-handed hewer were available, he could work close behind the right-hander, using an axe with the blade reversed, and the timber would be hewn in one operation.

Squaring was finished by rolling the log over onto one of the flat sides and making new lines, but this time with a cord impregnated with charcoal, so that the line was black. Then the scorers and hewers repeated their operations, with the result that the originally cylindrical log was changed to a square prism, with sharp or 'proud' angles. The same operation was used in squaring timbers for use in construction of houses and barns, and is the origin of the saying, 'Hew to the line and let the chips fall where they may'. As timber became more expensive, a slight reduction in waste was achieved by leaving rounded corners, instead of hewing to a sharp edge. Timber so squared was called waney.

In addition to the squared timbers for lumber, the British buyer also took unsquared pine trunks for ships' masts. Naturally the wood of these had to be of the finest quality. Some timbers of this sort were over 100 feet long.

RAFTING

The timber industry on the Ottawa River and its tributaries was a grand-scale operation until long after 1867. The gangs of lumbermen with their equipment moved into the logging areas by boat or road before the winter began. Each gang had its area of operation, and set up its camp as near the centre of this as possible. The main part of the camp was the shanty, a large log cabin with bunks and seats along two sides and one end. Heat for warmth and cooking was provided by a large fire in the centre of the floor, set on a fireplace of stones and sand. There was no chimney, the smoke escaping through a large hole in the roof. Until the 1860s the fire provided interior lighting as well, possibly helped by a few candles. Later, kerosene lanterns were widely used. Food was usually salt pork, beans, potatoes, and bread, with plenty of strong tea.

In addition to building the shanty, and shelters for the animals, the lumbermen cleared the roadways, and also made boats. Sometimes the boats could be brought back to the lumbering area from the previous run but more often these were sold and new ones built. The boats were used in assembling the timbers for the rafts, and as auxiliary craft during the run. They were a special type of craft, called 'bonne'. The bottom was flat from side to side but bowed upward fore and aft. The sides were inclined outward, and curved to a rakish point at either end. Propulsion was by both oar and paddle.

In constructing a raft the unit was the crib. This was made by selecting two timbers of equal length (40 to 50 feet) and drilling a 3-inch vertical hole near each end. Four-foot poles were set in these holes, and heavy, hand-hewn planks about 25 feet long were similarly drilled and dropped into place over the poles, so as to link the two timbers fore and aft. These transverse planks were called traverses. Additional traverses were added at intermediate points along the length of the timbers. Then additional floating timbers were pushed under the traverses to lie parallel with the side timbers and fill the intermediate area. If the last timber did not fit snugly, the extra space was taken up with wedges. The crib was finished by pulling three timbers onto the top of the traverses, one at the centre and one near each side, and securing them with poles set into the traverses. These were the 'loading sticks', and bore row-locks at the ends for the long oars or sweeps that helped to guide or propel the crib. Cribs were attached to each other by means of short, drilled planks called capping sticks, fitted over adjacent corner posts of two cribs. A full raft consisted of 100 or more cribs, but it could be separated quickly into single rows of cribs called bands for running rough water, or into individual cribs, by lifting the appropriate capping sticks. If necessary, even the cribs could be entirely dismantled and reassembled in an hour or two.

The crew, which might consist of fifty men, set up shelters of bark or boards on the cribs. The cook and his helpers had a proper shelter on a crib near the centre of the raft, with a fireplace built on a layer of sand. Some rafters preferred to have the culinary department travel in separate bonnes so as to be able to set up cooking and serving facilities in advance at the anchorage points.

84 Timber raft on the Ottawa river, c. 1880

Where the current was swift enough to carry the raft along, the sweeps served for steering, but in broad, slow stretches they were also used as oars. Small square sails could be hoisted to help speed progress. Sometimes it was necessary to throw out a kind of anchor called a kedge, and winch the raft forward by man-power. In later years small steam tugs towed the rafts along the slow stretches.

Originally it was necessary to dismantle the cribs completely at the very bad rapids such as the Chats and the Chaudière, but in 1828 Ruggles Wright, the son of Philemon, constructed a timber slide alongside the Chaudière Falls, wide enough to take a crib. By opening sluice gates at the top of the slide as the crib entered, sufficient water would go down with the crib to float it smoothly. Running the timber slide was exciting and somewhat dangerous, but it was a faster and easier way to pass the rapids than having to dismantle the raft completely and reassemble it below. Soon there were two slides at the Chaudière, one on each side, and others at the difficult rapids both upstream and down. On 1 September 1860, the Prince of Wales, afterwards Edward VII, rode with his entourage on a crib down the south timber slide at the Chaudière Falls. Remnants of this slide are still in existence.

Even with the slides it took several months to bring the timber rafts from the upper Ottawa to Quebec City. Here at Wolfe's Cove the timbers were inspected and graded. For the trip to Britain the timbers were loaded into ships directly from the cribs through loading ports in bow and stern, into which they were hoisted and pulled by cable and capstan.

As noted, the timber gathered in Lake Ontario came down as separate logs in runs. In the lake they were gathered in booms and built into relatively small rafts called drams. On the trip from Kingston to Montreal the rafts carried flour and other freight as well as the timber itself.

THE LUMBERMEN

The dangerous, strenuous, but relatively free life of the lumberman attracted a particular type of man, mostly from the French Canadian population of Lower Canada and New Brunswick. There were also numerous Irish, and some Iroquois Indians from Caughnawaga. Liquor was often brought into the camps, but as there was no way to spend wages there, the end of the run was marked by a period of carousing and fighting, sometimes between lumbermen and townsmen, but as often between French and

Irish. When the village of Bytown grew up at the mouth of the Rideau Canal, it became the first place 'outside' where the lumbermen could break loose, and for years the future capital of Canada looked forward with dread to the annual visitation of the raftsmen. Susanna Moodie, during her stay in Belleville, observed the French Canadian lumbermen each year as they brought the logs down the Moira River to Lake Ontario. She found them a brave, gay, rather admirable type, courteous when sober, but regrettably given to wild, drunken revels after the run was completed. Even in these they seem to have done no injury to the townspeople. The performance of the aquatic skills that their confrères of Ottawa put on for the Prince of Wales in 1860, and their ordered appearance and behaviour, were much admired both by the distinguished visitor and by the citizens of Ottawa.

LUMBER MILLING

As the timber trade with Britain declined during the middle years of the nineteenth century, a commerce in sawn lumber began to grow with the United States. Small saw-mills had been established early in the settlement, at suitable points on streams where dams and water-wheels could be set up. Most of these establishments were simple, with a single large saw blade mounted vertically, and coupled to the water-wheel so as to move rapidly up and down. The log to be sawn was set in a special frame, and moved forward on powered rollers. By adjusting the lateral position of the frame, any desired thickness of board could be sawed off as the log moved against the blade. The circular saw, a large steel disc with teeth, came into use during the 1850s. Later improvements were multiple-blade saws to cut several boards at once, and band-saws for fine cutting. Steam engines began to take the place of water-wheels as early as 1835.

Before the coming of the saw-mill, and long afterwards where a mill was not accessible, boards were sawn from logs by hand. This was usually done with a whip-saw, a long, flexible blade with a handle at each end. The log was mounted on a frame, and the boards were cut from it by the men, one on each side. A more efficient arrangement was the pit saw. The saw blade was operated vertically, the lower end projecting into a pit below the log bed, with one man above and one below to pull the saw. The man in the pit had a very unpleasant time, with scant air and lots of sawdust. Saws were also operated by horse treadmills and by 'horse-powers', the same devices that were used for powering threshing machines.

MAPLE SUGAR

A very different forest product was the sweetening obtained from the sap of the maple tree. The first-run sap of many trees contains sugar of some sort, but only the sugar-maple (*Acer saccharum*), a common tree in south-eastern Canada and the adjacent United States, has sap in sufficient quantity and sugar content to be the basis of an industry. Preparation of sugar from the maple-sap was discovered by the Indians, who passed on the technique to the colonists. They substituted iron kettles for clay pots. Until near the end of colonial times in Canada, imported cane sugar and molasses were expensive and of poor quality so the locally produced maple-sugar was an important source of sweetening.

In a normal spring the maple-sap would begin to ascend the trunks about the middle of March, but a warm spring could hasten the event and a cold spring delay it. The settler who would exploit his grove of maple trees or 'sugar bush' cleared narrow roads through the woods and set up a site for 'sugaring' near the middle of the area. Frosty nights and sunny days promote the maximum flow of sap. When a test boring revealed that the flow had started, the operator drilled a hole into the side of the trunk two or three feet above ground, and set into this a small wooden spout called a spile. During the day the sap ran in a constant drip from this spout. In the early days the liquid was collected in troughs carved out of some impervious wood and set under the drip. Later small buckets made of oak staves, like little kegs, were hung by wooden or wire handles from the spiles. During the height of the run the troughs or buckets were emptied once a day into a barrel drawn around the sugar bush on a sled pulled by oxen or horses. Back at the sugaring site the barrel was emptied into one or more large, hemispherical iron pots hung from a tripod or crane over a fire.

Once the sap began to boil it had to be watched day and night, to avoid it boiling over or evaporating dry. The boiling was controlled by moving the kettle away from the fire or by adding some fresh, cold sap. Bits of wood and other particles were skimmed off at this stage. When the quantity of liquid had been reduced by about half it was noticeably syrupy, and sweet to the taste. Now it was transferred to a wooden container and allowed to cool. Impurities that would not float settled out, and the liquid was poured off into another kettle, usually of copper. To make a first-quality sugar the syrup was then cleared. This was done by adding eggs or milk and bringing to a boil. The additive coagu-

85 Maple syrup bucket and maple sugar mould

86 The old method of making maple sugar: iron kettles over open fire. Bruce's Mill, Ontario

lated and absorbed impurities, and the solid matter was strained out. The final stage was the boiling of the syrup down to the desired concentration; this required even more careful supervision, as the thickening syrup could easily burn or boil over. The critical moment for pouring was determined by dropping a little of the syrup onto the snow. If it congealed to crystalline sugar it was ready. Another test was to dip a little loop of wire or a perforated strip of wood into the syrup, then hold it up and blow through the opening. If the syrup were thick enough a bubble of sugar would form. Following the Indian custom the early settlers poured the syrup into rectangular birch-bark containers, where it could solidify. Later, and especially in French Canada, wooden moulds carved in fanciful designs—hearts, faces, crescent moons, etc.—were used. Cast metal moulds eventually replaced the wooden moulds.

145

Samuel Strickland, who wrote a very good account of sugaring in pioneer days, mentioned some of the things that could happen to the inexperienced sugar maker. Besides having the sap boil over or the syrup burn because of the dereliction of a helper, Major Sam once had his cows get at the sap barrel and drink so much as to become badly bloated, only to be saved from a painful death by having their stomach walls punctured.

Final stages of the sugar making was an exciting time, especially for the children, who enjoyed the thrill of the critical operations and especially the very sweet toffee made by pouring the almost-finished syrup onto a plate of snow, from which it could be wound on a twig and eaten.

Towards the end of the run the sugar content of the sap fell off and the liquid was used to make vinegar rather than sugar. Boiled down to about one-fifth its original volume, it was placed in a cask with some yeast, and fermentation was allowed to take place. The addition of hops as well as yeast to the liquid produced a form of beer that was liked by some. By using the early, rich sap, and omitting the hops, a maple wine could be produced by controlled fermentation. As in other types of wine-making, the amount of sugar present made the difference between the production of wine or vinegar.

12

Hunting and Fishing

The European explorers and settlers of North America found everywhere a wealth of animal life on land and in the water. Rivers and lakes teemed with fishes, the sky was clouded with flights of birds, and the forests and prairies almost overrun with deer and bison. All this provided a readily available source of food. For many, the sport of hunting or fishing was an added attraction to the other advantages of settlement in the new country. The ubiquitous beaver and other fur-bearers offered wealth in the European fur markets, and much of the continent was penetrated and occupied in search of these furry treasures.

WEAPONS

The native peoples of North America, by the sixteenth and seventeenth centuries, had achieved a sort of balanced relationship with their wildlife environment. It may be that when they first invaded North America from Asia, at the closing of the Ice Age, they caused widespread destruction to some parts of the animal population. Eventually, however, an equilibrium had been established, in which people killed what they needed for food and clothing, and respected the wildlife as the source of their sustenance.

When the Europeans first encountered the native North Americans, the principal weapon of the latter was the bow. This was short compared with the English bow, and of composite construction with rawhide binding. The arrows were tipped with skilfully shaped heads of chalcedony or obsidian. The bow was held at an angle, rather than vertically, and the string was drawn with the thumb, in the Asiatic manner.

Had European man invaded North America before the fourteenth century, as indeed the Norsemen did in a small way, the conquest would have been much more protracted, for it would have been arrow against arrow. But by 1320 European inventors had discovered how to combine the ingredients of oriental fire-works—sulphur, nitre, and charcoal—so as to produce an explosive rather than a merely combustible powder. When this was placed in the closed end of a metal tube, and ignited through a narrow 'touch hole', the resultant explosion could propel a stone or metal ball from the tube with destructive velocity. So fire-arms were developed, at first for warfare, but later for hunting.

The fire-arms brought to Canada by Cartier and Champlain were primitive by later standards. They were the matchlock or arquebus, a heavy, clumsy weapon, which had to be supported on a forked stick for aiming and firing. The powder charge was ignited by means of a 'slow match', a piece of cord impregnated with potassium nitrate, which would retain a glowing end for a long time after being lit. This 'match' was clamped in a metal arm, which, at the right moment, could be pulled down to bring the glow in contact with the powder in the touch hole. There was little difference between firing an arquebus and a small cannon.

Such a weapon would be of little value in hunting, and even in warfare its main advantage over the bow was psychological. It was the invention of the much more practical flintlock that made fire-arms effective in hunting as well as in war. Fire-making by the impact of flint on steel had long been practised by Europeans, and by the middle of the seventeenth century the technique was being adapted for the discharge of fire-arms. The early devices were complicated and uncertain of operation, but by the end of the century the flintlock musket had reached a stage of development that was not surpassed for over 100 years.

The practical flintlock consisted of a hammer-like device, the head of which was a clamp, in which a chip of flint could be tightly gripped. The hammer was pivoted, and spring-loaded, so that it would swing forward, but an internal catch called a sear held it in the back or cocked position until released by a pull on the trigger. As the hammer snapped forward, it brought the flint chip in sharp contact with a steel plate called the frizzen, which was hinged to cover a small trough, the pan. Sparks struck from the vertical part of the frizzen showered into the pan as the frizzen was pushed away, and ignited the priming, a pinch of gunpowder. The flame entered the chamber of the musket through a small hole in the side, and fired the charge which expelled the bullet.

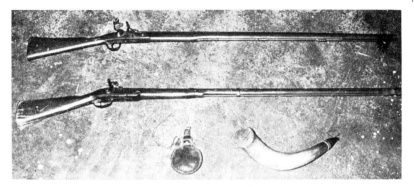

87 Flint-lock and percussion-cap rifles, powder flask and powder horn

The great majority of flintlock fire-arms had smooth, cylindrical barrels. Some were intended to discharge a cluster of small pellets, like the modern shotgun, and were called fowling-pieces. As the name suggests, they were used for shooting wild birds. The ordinary musket bullet was a cast lead ball, which fitted loosely into the barrel and was held by a paper wad. The accuracy of such a weapon was poor at distances over 100 yards, and in warfare great dependence was placed on volley firing. In hunting, however, it was necessary to approach the game close enough to ensure that the bullet would hit the point of aiming.

All this was changed by the introduction of the rifled barrel. It had long been known that a spinning projectile would travel farther and straighter than one which is simply pushing its way through the air. Putting spiral grooves or ridges on the inner surface of a fire-arm barrel was tried a number of times before a practical method of doing it was developed in the late eighteenth century. The rifled gun or rifle became the weapon of the individual marksman, in contrast to the volley-firing infantryman, and for this reason was especially adapted to hunting. The so-called Kentucky rifle, with its gracefully slender stock and extra long barrel, became the symbol of the American frontiersman. Actually this weapon was developed and manufactured in Lancaster County, Pennsylvania. As there was much emigration from this area to Upper Canada in the early 1800s, the long rifle or 'squirrel gun' was a familiar weapon on the Canadian as well as the American frontier.

The loose-fitting musket ball was useless in a rifled barrel, as the spiral grooves had to grip the bullet to impart the rotary motion. A tight-fitting ball could be used if hammered down the barrel into place, but this was a tedious operation. With the American rifle the problem was solved by using a patch of cloth about one inch square; this was pushed slightly into the muzzle, then the ball dropped into the little pocket so formed, and the patch and ball rammed home together. The cloth between bullet and barrel provided the tight fit needed to transmit the rotary motion.

A new era in fire-arms was begun in 1807 with the invention of the percussion cap. As eventually developed, this consisted of a tiny copper cap which fitted over a nipple-like tube that took the place of the flint-lock pan. The hammer was reduced to a simple head, designed to strike the top of the copper cap. Under this top was a pinch of mercury fulminate, a compound so unstable that a moderate impact causes it to explode. The flash from the explosion travelled down the nipple tube and ignited the charge in the chamber. This method of discharging a fire-arm was not only simpler and more dependable, but could be substituted for the flint-lock without a major conversion of the weapon. Nevertheless it was near the middle of the nineteenth century before military establishments completed the change to the new method. But hunters recognized the value of the percussion cap very early; in addition to its greater simplicity and dependability, it could be used in wet weather, when the powder in a flint-lock pan could easily become too damp to ignite.

Fine hunting rifles in the Pennsylvania tradition were made in Upper Canada in the early 1800s, but they were too expensive for the average settler. A heavier but useful weapon became available in the 1850s, the British Enfield rifle, which was issued to members of the Militia, and was available between periods of service for civilian purposes.

The final step in the development of the modern rifle was the introduction of the breech-loading mechanism. Even the most up-to-date muzzle-loader required that a measured charge of powder be poured down the barrel, then the bullet and its wad forced down on top of the charge by means of the ramrod. It was an operation that was best done in a standing position, which might be a disadvantage in both hunting and war. As early as 1776, Lieutenant-Colonel Patrick Ferguson of the British Army had invented a practical breech-loading flint-lock musket, the adoption of which would have changed history, but the inventor was killed at the battle of King's Mountain, North Carolina, in 1780. It was not until the introduction of the metal cartridge, holding bullet, powder, and percussion cap in one container, that the breech-loading rifle became popular. By the 1860s the British Enfield rifle was being converted by installing the Snider breech block, a cylinder which could be swung out to open the breech for the cartridge and swung back to close the breech for firing.

GAME

Settlers in the Atlantic colonies or the Canadas found the white-tailed deer to be the commonest large mammal, and the easiest to hunt. These deer are solitary in habit, although in winter they gather in small herds when the snow becomes deep, and form trampled 'yards' where they can find some food and shelter. They are easiest to hunt in the autumn, after the leaves have fallen, and when a light snow may reveal their tracks. Hunting these deer has not changed much since pioneer times. Unless following a trail, the hunter simply walks through the woods, watching for movement or listening for the tell-tale snap of a twig. It is best to walk against the wind, as deer can detect the scent of men at a distance. On sighting a deer the hunter must get off his shot before his prey takes alarm. Even with modern fire-arms there is seldom time for a second shot. If the deer does not fall, it may still be mortally wounded. In the days of black powder and muzzle-loading fire-arms this was a common situation, and the hunter had to follow the trail of blood spots, perhaps for miles, until the final collapse of the deer occurred. Deer incline to be creatures of habit, and have their favourite feeding or drinking places. Hunters who knew these took up position near them, especially in the late afternoon, when the air was still and the animals active. Dogs were sometimes used to hunt deer, flushing them out of hiding for the shot, and following a wounded animal more swiftly than the hunter could. Stalking deer required intense concentration, and the tension built up might make an inexperienced hunter so nervous that he would be unable to shoot when the quarry was sighted. This condition occurred so commonly that it had its own name: buck fever.

The much larger moose kept farther away from settlements, and hunting it required long trips from home. The hunting methods were much the same as for deer, except that in the autumn the male moose could be lured into rifle range by imitating the call of the female moose, using a roll of birch bark as a trumpet.

The western plains, from the Red River Valley to the Rocky

Mountains, were the home of vast herds of bison ('buffalo'), which were the basis of the way of life of the plains Indians. This was partly adopted by the French and Métis who were employed by the fur-trading companies in the vicinity of Fort Garry, but not by the Scottish settlers of the Red River colony, who preferred farming and trading. The annual buffalo hunt was a great event, involving numerous hunters who travelled in trains of Red River carts, and camped on the prairie, Indian-fashion. When a herd was located it was followed by the whole brigade. Killing the animals was usually done by stalking, less frequently by the dangerous running method, in which the hunter on a swift pony rode alongside his prey at full gallop and despatched it with a shot from a short-barrelled musket. Hides were the main object of the hunt; they not only provided leather and blankets for the hunters, but were useful for trade. The tongues, a delicacy, were eaten by the hunters, and some of the meat was preserved by drying or making into pemmican.

Wolves were hunted, not only because of their attacks on sheep and young cattle, but also because of the possibility that they might attack humans, especially women and children. For many years a bounty was paid for each wolf killed, this being claimed by presentation of the scalp to a magistrate. Black bears, although more formidable than wolves, were seldom a threat to humans or domestic animals, but they were hunted for their fur, and sometimes for their meat, which, in young individuals at least, is delicious.

TRAPPING

Important as was the hunting of animals for food, the killing of fur-bearing mammals for their pelts was the purpose of much of the European penetration of the Canadian region. Of these, the beaver was by far the most important. Excellent as are the garments made from the tanned hides of the beaver, with their soft, dense fur, it was the use of this fur in making felt for hats that created the great demand in the seventeenth and eighteenth centuries.

The native people killed beaver in moderation for their warm furs and for the fleshy tails which they considered a delicacy. The advent of the Europeans, who would exchange knives, axes, pots, and even guns for the beaver pelts, led to widespread slaughter of beaver by the natives. Their methods were crude, involving total destruction of the colonies. The way of life of the beaver is unique.

It feeds on the tender bark of deciduous trees, which it fells by gnawing with its powerful incisor teeth. Some beaver live in burrows in the banks of streams, the entrance below water level, but mostly they build 'houses' of sticks and mud in ponds which they create by damming streams with logs and brush. Although the entrance to the house is below water level, the living quarters inside are well above, and there is an opening for air in the top. In winter the beavers spend most of their time in the houses, coming out for brief excursions under the ice to gather the green sticks that they have sunk in the pond before the freeze-up.

It was at this time, when the fur was prime, and the beaver colonies most vulnerable, that the native hunters took their toll. After locating the entrance to the house, the hunters placed nets through the ice in front, then chopped into the house from above. Those beaver that tried to escape were netted, and the others were caught in the house. Another method was to break through the dam, allowing water to escape and the level to fall. The beaver rushing to repair the damage were then netted.

The Europeans brought the steel trap to North America at an early date. This ingenious device has changed little in three centuries. It consists of a pair of iron or steel jaws, with or without teeth, which are hinged on each other at the ends. In the unset position the jaws are held tightly closed by one or two steel springs. These are U-shaped straps of steel, the lower arm of which is attached to the trap base, and the upper arm encircles the sides of the jaws in a loop. By compressing the spring the jaws can be opened to a horizontal position, where they are held in place by a hinged strip of metal over one jaw, hooked to a catch on a trigger or pan in the centre of the trap. The arrangement is the same as in the familiar mousetrap, but on a larger, more powerful, scale.

In the trapping of flesh-eating mammals, some sort of bait was usually attached to the pan of the trap. With beaver, however,

88 Wrought iron trap, c. 1840. Woodbridge, Ontario

the method was different. The trap was set under water, with a lure such as a tender stick supported over it. Use was often made of a glandular extract from the beaver, called castoreum, the odour of which masked the scent of men, and provided an irresistible lure for the beaver. Some arrangement of the trap was made so that the beaver, once caught, could not come to the surface, and was drowned. This might be done by attaching a heavy log to the trap, or by looping the trap chain over a stick, with stubs of branches on it pointing down, so that the chain could be pulled down but not up again.

Beavers were skinned flat, that is, with a cut the full length of the under side and up each leg. The frame for stretching and drying the pelt was made by bending and tying a willow branch in an oval shape. Then a thong was laced through holes made near the edge of the pelt, and over the willow frame. When the thong was pulled tight, the hide was stretched as a smooth, taut surface within the frame. Scraped of all traces of fat, the hide in the frame was hung up to dry. Later it was removed from the frame and sold to the trader as a stiff, flat skin. He, in turn, pressed the skins into bundles for shipping.

Other fur-bearing mammals that were trapped for their skins were the fox, the mink and the otter. Along the northern Pacific coast there was, in the eighteenth and early nineteenth century, a flourishing trade in the skins of the sea otter, a marine mammal which could be taken with gun or net. Fabulous prices were paid by the Chinese for this fur, and the animal was brought almost to extinction. All of these mammals were skinned in the 'cased' form, that is, the skin was cut only across the rump and hind legs. The body being long and narrow, the skin could then be peeled forward over the trunk and head to form a long, narrow sleeve, with the fur inside. After cleaning, it was stretched over a narrow, flat blade of wood whittled to the proper shape.

SEAL HUNTING

The Gulf of St Lawrence and the sea north of Newfoundland were, and still are, the scene of the spectacular seal hunt. Two species were involved, the harp seal and the hooded seal. These come down from Davis Strait, in the autumn, to winter in more southern waters. In the early spring the females have their young ('pups') on the floe ice. At first the coastal settlers went out on the ice and killed the seals, dragging them back to shore. Later they used boats to cross open water, and from this the hunt evolved into a great annual event, in which a fleet of ships set out from St John's and sailed north into the ice-fields until herds of 'swiles' were sighted. Then most of the crew went over the side onto the ice, armed with gaff or gun, and carrying a skinning knife, rope, and compass. The harp seals were killed with blows of the gaff, but the hooded seals had to be shot. Then the skin was removed, leaving on it the thick layer of fat, and the accumulated skins were dragged over the ice to the ship. Here the fat was scraped from the hides and 'rendered', that is, heated in vats to separate the valuable oil. The skins were dried, to be used later for the making of fine leather. Back in harbour the oil was boiled with water, to remove impurities, and bleached by sunlight, to achieve the preferred pale colour. Until the 1860s, seal oil was an important lamp fuel in the eastern colonies, and was also used in food and as a lubricant.

The annual seal hunt was an important part of the economy of Newfoundland, providing cash for communities and individuals who lived mostly under the credit system. Profits of the hunt were distributed as shares to owners, captain and crew, but they varied with the catch, and sometimes ships were crushed in the ice, or men lost in prolonged fog. Steam vessels replaced sailing ships in the 1860s; fewer were needed, but the actual catch was larger. The work was arduous and dangerous, and the reward uncertain, but the excitement of the hunt, almost as much as the pay, drew full crews to the sealing fleet each year.

WHALING

Sealing was for Newfoundland what whaling was for the coastal parts of the New England states. Nova Scotia and New Brunswick, with a strong seafaring tradition, never did get deeply involved in either enterprise. In the 1830s the port of Saint John, New Brunswick, sent a number of whaling vessels to the South Pacific, and the returns for a time were spectacular. But ships were lost, and the whales became scarce, and by the 1840s the maritime interests of the New Brunswickers turned to overseas trade; and their sailing ships, along with those of Nova Scotia, rivalled the fleets of England and the United States in voyages made and commerce carried.

FISHING

Long before the abundance of furs was suspected, Europeans were coming to North America for its prodigious wealth of fishes. News of the Cabot voyages of 1497 and 1498 may have been the trigger, but the advent of English, French, and Portuguese fishermen on the Grand Banks was so soon after as to suggest that perhaps they were there first. In the interior of the continent the rivers and lakes teemed with fishes, a ready source of food for the settlers and an added fillip of sport for the gentleman farmer. The annual run of salmon in the rivers of the northern Pacific coast formed the basis of elaborate native cultures before the coming of the fur trader, and as settlements grew, provided a rival industry to farming and mining.

The native people fished with nets woven from fibres of bark. Spearing was widely used. These methods were modified or augmented by the European settlers. Nets were of many types, adapted to the circumstances and the needs of the fisherman. For simple home consumption the dip net might be adequate, so heavy were the runs of fish on occasion. More common, however, was the seine, a kind of barricade net stretched across a stream, in which the fish became entangled. Sometimes the catch was so great as to break the net. In large streams or along the shores of lakes where currents were strong, weirs were built, barricades that turned the runs of fish shoreward into a pen, from which they were readily taken by net. The fish-trap or fyke was often used, a closed net with a tapered opening into which the fish could swim readily, but from which they could not escape.

Spearing fish was not a way of commercial fishing, but it had an element of skill and excitement that attracted both native and white man. It was done at night, from a boat with a light suspended at the bow. This might be a fire in an iron basket called a jack light, or later an oil or kerosene flare. The spears used by the settlers were tridents, with prongs about six inches long. The centre prong had a double-barbed head, the outer ones with barbs only on the inner side.

Few Candian settlers had the time or the need for the elaborate rituals of fly-fishing so dear to the followers of Isaak Walton. They simply tied a barbed iron hook onto the end of a linen cord, and fastened the other end to a freshly-cut pole. Bait might be a worm, a bit of meat, or even a tuft of red cloth. Officers stationed with British regiments in Canada used the sophisticated equipment of flies, reels, and bamboo rods, but it seems unlikely that they caught more fish.

Cod fishing on the Newfoundland Banks was a true harvest of the sea. Each year the ships came out from the ports of western

Europe. First there were the tiny caravels, with lateen sails. Then came the dogger boats, originating in the Netherlands, which were two-masted and partly square-rigged. Finally the schooner, a New England invention, became the predominant craft. It had low, clean lines, with two or three masts, on which square sails were combined with fore-and-aft sails.

The early years of the fisheries were times of improvisation. The catch was salted and carried back to the home port for drying. But it was obvious that a more efficient method would be to establish temporary stations at convenient harbours on the Newfoundland coast and complete the processing there, after which the dried fish could be tightly packed for the voyage home. There was much rivalry for the better harbours, but eventually areas of influence were recognized. The French bases were on the south-east, along Placentia Bay, but their establishments, except for one or two forts, were seasonal. The English, who chose the Avalon Peninsula and the magnificent harbour of St John's, exercised their well-known habit of forming permanent settlements. These were overrun and destroyed by the French in 1696, but were soon rebuilt, and in 1713 it was the turn of the French to surrender all territorial claims, leaving only certain vague rights to use Placentia Bay as a base for their fisheries.

As a result of these events the French, along with the Portuguese and the Basques, remained more or less dependent on their European ports, while the English fisheries became almost entirely based on Newfoundland. This did not make much difference to the actual techniques of fishing. The fish were taken by baited hook and line, operated by individual crewmen working from the sides of the ship. In the caravels and dogger boats they were stationed on platforms built out over the sides, but in the schooners they worked directly from the deck. When the fisherman played out his line with baited hook to suitable depth, he jerked it up and down quickly, giving the bait a 'jigging' motion. Almost immediately a fish was hooked, to be hauled in hand-over-hand and pulled on board with a gaff hook or a landing net. Cutting up the catch went on simultaneously with the fishing, and the tongues were set aside, not just as delicacies, but as tally for each man's catch, for a portion of the profits from the total haul went to each member of the crew in proportion to his contribution to it.

A great revolution in cod fishing came about in 1789 with the invention of 'long-line' fishing. This originated with the French. The equipment consisted of a stout line about 100 feet long, to each end of which was attached a cork float. Along the line, at regular intervals, other lines were attached at right angles, and these lines bore hooks. The fishermen would put out one float, then successively bait each hook and cast it over as they played out the main line. When the other float was cast off, the result would be a line more or less horizontally suspended in the water, with a series of lines with baited hooks hanging vertically from it. So abundant were the fish that the fishermen could row back to the starting end and begin pulling in the catch and rebaiting the hooks as soon as the whole line was laid out.

Long-line fishing was carried out at first from long boats, with several men to row and to set the line. A more efficient method was introduced about 1825, with the use of dories. These were small boats that could be manned readily by one or two men, easily launched, and conveniently stacked on deck when not in use. Fishing from dories is dangerous, however, and today is practised only by the Portuguese. The small boats could easily be lost in fog, or swamped by heavy seas. The latter was most likely to happen when the doryman was trying to make his way back to the schooner with a heavy load of fish.

A major part of preparing for cod fishing was the gathering of the bait. Herring was a commonly used bait, being taken in nets offshore, and often in such quantities that the excess could be sold to the larger ships, especially those from foreign ports. An even richer source, on occasion, was the capelin, a small, smelt-like fish that comes ashore in vast numbers at some times of the year. The favourite bait, however, was the squid. These were obtained by a technique known as jigging. A 'squid-jigger' is a small lead weight in which is set a circle of sharp hooks pointing upward. It is painted bright red to attract the squids. In jigging for squid, the jigger is attached to a line and lowered over the side of a boat where squid are likely to occur. The line is given a quick up-and-down action, and this 'jigging' of the bright lure attracts the squid which becomes caught on the hooks and is hauled on board. During a good run of squid a dory can be filled in an hour or less.

The runs of herring, capelin, and squid are seasonal, and in the early days, in the off season, fishing either ceased, or depended for bait on the entrails of the fish already caught. Then the French fishermen hit on the idea of using the whelk, a large marine snail, which is available all year. This made them independent of the bait fishermen of Newfoundland, who were not always able or willing to supply the required amounts of bait.

The Treaty of Paris in 1763, by which France lost much of her territory in North America, left under French rule the tiny islands of St Pierre and Miquelon, off the south-east coast of Newfoundland, and some vague rights to use harbours in Placentia Bay. By the second Treaty of Paris, 1783, those rights were transferred to the west coast of Newfoundland, which became known as the French Shore.

The fishing vessels based on European ports usually preserved their catch by packing the cleaned fish in casks with salt. But the Newfoundland ships brought their fish to harbour, where they were eviscerated and split into triangular slabs, which were stacked in vats with layers of salt. This salting took about eight days, after which the fish were washed and laid out on rocks, or platforms, to dry in the sun. At many of the rocky harbours the racks had to be supported on elaborate frames known as flakes. The usual procedure was to spread the cod to dry each morning, and remove it to shelter each evening. This went on for about a week. The partially-dried fish were then piled for a week or two, after which the daily drying was resumed for another few days. Cod fish so salted and dried was almost imperishable, and was the major, almost exclusive product of the Newfoundland settlements. The word 'fish' meant cod fish, other kinds always being specifically named.

Like all one-crop economies, the Newfoundland cod fishery was subject to its ups and downs. A poor catch left the fisherman in debt to the local merchant, who still had to supply the needs of the next season's fishing, as well as the necessities of life for the man and his family. A good catch did little more than pay off debts and start a new cycle. The merchants themselves were often ruined by a series of bad years, for they in turn operated on credit from the major suppliers. So over the years the economy of Newfoundland became a system of debts, and more and more the larger companies obtained control of the fisheries. It was well into the latter half of the nineteenth century before lumbering and mining became important enough to diversify the economy and provide an alternative to fishing as a means of livelihood.

13

Transportation

For many years the most important means of travel in the French and British colonies was by water. Unlike the eastern United States, where navigable stretches of the rivers are short, and mostly run from the north rather than the west, Canada is traversed by large east-west rivers and lakes, which facilitated penetration of the continent from the Atlantic to the Rocky Mountains and beyond.

The greatest of these waterways is the St Lawrence system, which includes the Great Lakes. Today these waters are linked by a series of canals, and ocean-going vessels can travel from the Gulf of St Lawrence to the head of Lake Superior, a distance of over 1,800 miles. Originally, however, Montreal was the head of oceanic navigation, and large sailing ships were a common sight in its harbour long after the colonial period. This is not to say that sailing up the great river was easy, for ships often had to wait days at Quebec for a favourable wind.

Commencing with the Lachine Rapids immediately above Montreal, there is a series of rapids that formed barricades to early river travel. The Lachine Rapids act as a dam to produce a broad expanse of quiet water above, known as Lake St Louis. It is into this that the major tributary, the Ottawa River, enters at Perrot Island by two branches. Not far above this are the Cedar Rapids, about 10 miles long, which produce another stretch of quiet water, Lake St Francis.

Until the construction in recent years of the St Lawrence Seaway, the most formidable of all these rapids was the Long Sault, at the head of Lake St Francis. These rapids were over 11 miles long, and although navigable by special craft with experienced crews, they took a heavy toll of the early traffic. It was here in 1758 that General Amherst, on his way to besiege Montreal, lost a large number of men by the wrecking of boats with inexperienced crews. Today the site of this great cataract lies beneath the calm waters of Lake St Lawrence, formed by the flooding above the Long Sault dam.

Above the Long Sault there were other less impressive rapids, but from the Thousand Islands westward, navigation of the river was easy. At Kingston the river opens into Lake Ontario, 160 miles of open water on which the only danger is the sudden storm. This was partly avoided by skirting the north shore, behind a chain of islands, and entering the winding Bay of Quinte. At the head of this is the narrow neck of land known as the Carrying Place, near the present town of Trenton. Crossing this barrier, the traveller found himself again on open water, with about a third of the lake by-passed.

The greatest barrier to shipping on the St Lawrence waterway was formed by the gorge and falls of the Niagara River, through which the water of Lake Erie descends some 350 feet to Lake Ontario. Only by a climb up the escarpment and a 13-mile road trip to Chippewa Creek, could travellers and cargoes pass from the lower to the upper navigable stretches of the river.

The Niagara River leads into Lake Erie, and from here navigation is uninterrupted to the head of the lake, thence up the Detroit River to Lake St Clair, and up the St Clair River to Lake Huron. About 250 miles of lake travel brings shipping to the entrance to Lake Michigan, and through this route the early explorers penetrated into the Mississippi Valley. For the far west, however, it was necessary to pass the Sault Ste Marie, the rapids of St Mary. Above these is Lake Superior, the largest of all the lakes, 450 miles to the tip at the present city of Duluth, or 300 miles to the start of the Grand Portage, over which by a series of rivers, lakes, and carrying trails, the traveller crossed the height of land and descended into the Red River Valley. An alternative route, more removed from the International Boundary, was by way of the Kaministiquia River. The present city of Thunder Bay lies at the entrance to this route.

The French explorers out of Montreal had a shorter if somewhat more strenuous way of by-passing the Niagara barrier. This was the Ottawa River route, which was later used by the North West Fur Trading Company. Turning up the Ottawa at Ste Anne's, the travellers encountered a number of rapids and falls, but these were all short enough to be by-passed by walking and carrying.

Near the site of the present town of Mattawa, where the direction of the valley turns north, the travellers worked their way up a tributary stream and overland into Lake Nipissing. From here the route was down the French River to Georgian Bay, the north-east arm of Lake Huron. Keeping to a passage between the north shore of the lake and a series of islands, it was possible to reach the Sault Ste Marie with protection from the storms of the open lake.

Another way of by-passing the Niagara barrier was to work one's way north-westward from Lake Ontario. The most commonly used route was that which came to be called the Trent Waterway. This began at the head of the Bay of Quinte, and by a series of rivers and lakes, with obstructions, gave access to Lake Simcoe. From here the Severn River led into Georgian Bay. Another way to Lake Simcoe was up the Humber River just west of the site of Toronto. This involved a lengthy overland trip from the head of navigation to the lake, but there were no steep gradients.

The Hudson's Bay Company set up establishments on the west coast of Hudson Bay in the seventeenth century, but eventually found it necessary to push inland to meet the competition of traders from Montreal. There was a choice of two routes. The more southerly was up the Nelson River to Lake Winnipeg. From here the traders could travel south to the mouth of the Red River and upstream to Fort Garry and Red River settlement. Alternatively they could turn westward, up the Saskatchewan River, and travel to the edge of the Rocky Mountains. The more northerly route was up the Churchill River, a long, winding waterway of alternating rapids and lakes, to the vicinity of the present boundary between Saskatchewan and Alberta. A short but strenuous overland trip on the Methy Portage led to the Clearwater River. Descending this to the Athabaska River, the travellers had a clear run to Lake Athabaska. Here the Slave River starts, but a few miles downstream is the junction with the Peace River, and up this the westward route turned. There were no serious barriers on this stream for 600 miles to the edge of the Rocky Mountains. The Peace River is the only major stream that rises on the west side of the main Rocky Mountain range. Here it is formed by two tributaries, the Finley River from the north and the Parsnip River from the south. By going up the Parsnip, it was possible to cross the height of land into the headwaters of the Fraser River, and go down it to the Pacific Ocean. This was the route followed by Alexander Mackenzie and Simon Fraser. Alternately, one could go up the Fraser, cross over into the headwaters of the Columbia River, and thence travel by either that stream or the shorter Kootenay River, to the mouth of the Columbia near the site of the present city of Portland, Oregon. These were the routes explored by David Thompson.

CANALS

Although the usual method of by-passing the rapids, or falls, of the waterways was by walking or carrying over the so-called portages, it was obvious from early colonial times that many of these barriers could be circumvented by means of some sort of canal. Under the French régime, efforts were made to by-pass the Lachine Rapids above Montreal, but this project was only brought to a practical conclusion under British rule, when the military engineers completed a narrow canal in 1779. A more practical canal, 20 feet wide and 5 feet deep, with locks, was built in 1825. Meanwhile, in 1798, the North West Fur Trading Company had made a canal past the Sault Ste Marie, so that their boats could go from Lake Huron to Lake Superior. The Niagara was by-passed by the Welland Canal opened in 1829, completed 1839. The organizer and principal director of this enterprise was William H. Merritt of St Catherine's. Using Twelve-Mile Creek as the entrance to the canal, a series of locks was built to raise boats to the top of the escarpment. From here it was easy to connect to Chippawa Creek and the Niagara River. Merritt went on to take a leading part in the construction of canals along the St Lawrence River, and by the 1840s it was possible for a ship to pass from Lake Huron to tidewater at Montreal.

Previous to this, the best way for larger craft to reach Lake Ontario from Montreal was through the Rideau Canal. This was built by Royal Engineers under Lt.-Col. John By, in 1832–1836. Planned originally from military considerations, this canal was for a time a very important commercial artery. By means of a canal by-passing the Long Sault of the Ottawa, craft of medium size ascended the Ottawa River to the vicinity of the Chaudière Falls, at the site of the present city of Ottawa. Here by a series of locks they climbed to the Rideau River and travelled southward up that stream, with numerous small locks, to the Rideau Lakes. From these, short canals led into the Lake Ontario drainage and thence to the lake at Kingston. In this way both the rapids of the

89 The original Welland Canal, St Catherine's, Ontario

St Lawrence and the vulnerable international stretch of that river were by-passed.

WATER CRAFT

The European settlers of what was to be Canada found the native people travelling on the numerous waterways in a variety of craft. To these the name canoe (pronounced 'kannoo') was generally applied. This was the name acquired by the Spanish discoverers from the people that they encountered, and passed on to other Europeans. The Canadian region had three types of canoes, differing in materials, construction, and seaworthiness.

Least sophisticated was the dugout canoe. It was made by hollowing out a large log, usually of cedar, to form a semi-circular trough about ten or twelve feet long, and three feet in width. The ends were pointed to form bow and stern. Before the coming of the Europeans, the hollowing was done with stone tools, or by burning and scraping. Later, steel axes and adzes made the task much quicker. In the Great Lakes region, and in the Rocky Mountains, dugout canoes were used well into the nineteenth century. They were simple to make, and strong enough to stand rough use, but they were none too stable in the water, and they were too heavy to be carried far overland. On the Pacific Coast, where the great Douglas firs were available, dugout canoes were made with a length of over 20 feet. With graceful lines, and a high bow and stern, they were not unlike the dragon ships of the Norse sea raiders, and were used for much the same purposes. With a crew of 20 or more paddlers, they navigated the coastal waters from Alaska to Puget Sound.

The elm-bark canoe was a common craft in the Great Lakes region. To make it, an elm log about 10 feet long and two or three feet in diameter was slit longitudinally, so that the bark could be peeled off in one cylindrical roll. The edges at the ends were then brought together to form a vertical seam, which was sewn together with thin strips of cedar bark, and sealed with pine resin. The longitudinal edges between the two end seams were then pulled apart, and held in the spread position by sticks serving as crude thwarts. Such a canoe could be made quickly, but it was unstable, easily damaged, and difficult to repair. Usually it was made for just one trip, and abandoned at the conclusion. Many tribes, even the great Iroquois Confederacy, used the elm-bark canoe almost exclusively.

The third type, the birch-bark canoe, was so widely and successfully used that it came to be what most people meant by the word canoe. Copied in modern materials, such as canvas, aluminium, or fibre-glass, it is still a popular water-craft for sport and travel. In its original form it was especially characteristic of the Algonquin tribes of the central woodlands, from whom it was obtained by the early explorers and fur traders.

To build a birch-bark canoe the craftsman first drove into the ground a double row of stakes in the horizontal shape of the hull, and projecting up about as high as the future gunwales. The latter were then outlined by lashing to the stakes a row of cedar splints. Ribs were fashioned from strips of ash, bent in a U-shaped curve to make the shape of the hull from side to side. To keep the framework from collapsing a series of thwarts was then fitted; these were straight slats reaching from one rim to the other. When these were secured by bindings, the skeleton of the canoe was complete, and it was removed from the stakes and turned over for application of the birch bark.

The bark was peeled from the birch trees during the winter months, when it was dry. Sometimes the canoe builder marked a suitable tree in the summer, so that others would leave the bark for him to use when the time came. Sheets, free from defects and as wide as could be conveniently handled, were peeled from the tree. These were wrapped over the inverted framework of the canoe, and sewn to the ribs and gunwales with cedar fibres. The edges of adjacent sheets of bark were also united by stitching. All seams and holes were then sealed with some tarry substance, usually the heated pitch of the pine tree.

Modern canoes have only a moderate rise of the gunwales to bow and stern, but the old-time birch-bark canoes had these ends elevated into a high, graceful, slightly recurved outline. This helped to avoid shipping water when the canoe was running rapids, or driving against the wind in open water. For ordinary use birch-bark canoes were ten to fifteen feet long, but the freight canoes used by the fur brigades were 25 or more feet in length. These were called master canoes, *canots de maître*. Even these giants were light enough to be lifted and carried over portages. If the bark sheathing were punctured or split by striking against stones, it could be repaired with birch-bark patches, and pine pitch obtained on the spot.

Transporting the canoes and their contents around impassable rapids or over heights of land was a normal part of canoe travel. A small canoe was carried by one man, who swung it up to an inverted position over his shoulders, with one of the thwarts resting on his back. Arms balancing the load, and head inside the canoe, the portager struggled along the partly cleared trail from landing to launching place. The contents of the canoe, equipment, supplies, or furs, were carried on separate trips or by other members of the party. Portaging the big fur brigades was a major operation, but the crews were large. Loads of 90 pounds were standard for each man, but by using the tump line, a leather band extending from the load around the forehead, weights of 150 pounds or more were carried. The great canoes required six to eight men for carrying, with perhaps an extra man in front to guide the load around obstructions.

For transportation on the St Lawrence River the freight canoe was not large enough for the loads required nor strong enough to survive the dragging up the rapids. So a type of boat came into use which was known under various spellings as the bateau. It was 30 to 40 feet long, and five to eight feet wide at midlength, but narrowing to a pointed end at bow and stern. The bottom was flat, which provided a shallow draught, and permitted beaching on a rocky shore. For propulsion oars were normally used, but up a strong current the crew pushed the craft with poles. In rapids, a rope might be attached and pulled from shore, or the crew might wade, and guide the boat around the rocks. In open water, a single triangular sail was hoisted, using one of the oars as a mast.

Until well into the nineteenth century the bulk of cargoes on the St Lawrence River between Montreal and Kingston was carried in these bateaux. Many of the settlers who came to Upper Canada during the great period of British immigration had their belongings transported in this fashion, and perhaps travelled in the bateaux themselves. But it was an uncomfortable mode, and some like Samuel Strickland found it more convenient to walk part of the way, and pick up their property at Kingston. The crews were almost invariably French Canadians, hard workers who sang and cursed with equal readiness. The leader of the crew manned the oar that served as tiller, and his orders were obeyed instantly, as all relied on his experience and judgment for a safe passage.

A somewhat larger type of boat came into use in the nineteenth century. This was the Durham boat, up to 90 feet in length, and provided with a slip keel to give better stability under sail without greatly increasing the draught. The mast was a permanent fixture, but propulsion was usually by means of oars.

In 1823 the Hudson's Bay Company abandoned the freight canoe as its principal means of transporting supplies and furs. A new craft, the York boat, was introduced on the Great Lakes,

90 The only surviving York boat. Lower Fort Garry, Manitoba

and especially on Lake Winnipeg and its rivers. This was a keeled vessel, about 50 feet long, and capable of carrying a square sail even in adverse weather conditions. This was made possible not only by the lines, but also by the stout mast, and the arrangement for raising and lowering the sail quickly. Extensive use of this craft followed the construction of canals to by-pass those rapids up which it could not be lined.

The construction of sailing ships, large enough and stout enough to put to sea, began in Canada under the French régime in the 1660s. They were known as King's Ships, owned by the government and used primarily for military purposes but also available for civil transportation. This arrangement was continued under British rule, and it was not until settlement began in Upper Canada that privately-owned merchant ships appeared on the Great Lakes. Most of these were small, the schooner being the usual type. This had two masts, mostly fore-and-aft rigged, but possibly with one or two square sails on the foremast. A similar vessel but with both masts square-rigged was called a brig. Larger than either of these was the bark with three masts, the foremast and mainmast square-rigged.

A curious craft much used as a ferry on short runs was the horse boat. On this a pair of paddle wheels were turned by horse power, the horses operating a treadmill or turning a windlass-like device similar to those used for powering threshing machines and saws.

The first practical steamboat was launched by Robert Fulton on the Hudson River in 1808. Two years later John Molson established a steamship run between Montreal and Quebec with his little paddle-wheeler *Accommodation*. The *Frontenac*, a schooner-rigged steamship, was the first on Lake Ontario, being launched at Ernestown (Bath) in 1816. The first steam vessel on Lake Erie was launched on the American shore near Buffalo in 1818; this was the *Walk-on-water*. It then became possible to travel by steamboat from Kingston to Detroit, with the 13-mile overland interruption between Queenston and Chippawa which was traversed by wagon or stagecoach.

ROADS

The development of roads was late in British North America because the waterways provided a cheaper, quicker, and more comfortable means of travel. But even under the French régime a start was made on a highway system. The Royal Road, between Quebec and Montreal, was completed in 1733.

Soon after Colonel Simcoe established a provincial government in Upper Canada in 1792, he began planning trunk roads. He was greatly impressed with the country west of Lake Ontario, for he realized its rich agricultral potential. So in 1793 he authorized the construction of Dundas Street. This was named for the then Secretary of State in Britain, and was intended to link Lake Ontario with the Detroit area. However, when in the same year the provincial capital was transferred from Newark (Niagara) to York (Toronto), settlement began to spread northward towards Lake Simcoe. Short sections of a crude road had already been hacked out of the woods by the settlers when official construction of a highway was begun in 1795. The initial cutting was by the Queen's Rangers, and was pushed through the 33 miles to navigable water near Lake Simcoe by early 1796. The road was named Yonge Street, after the British Minister of War. It was some years before this artery was improved enough to justify its existence, the start being made in 1799 when the North West Fur Trading Company decided to haul their boats from Lake Ontario to Lake Simcoe over this route.

The line between York and Kingston was also started as local sections before an overall plan was adopted. First work on the trunk road was undertaken by Asa Danforth, and the resultant highway became known as the Danforth Road. This name is preserved in Danforth Avenue in Toronto, along with Dundas Street and Yonge Street. By 1801 a road of sorts existed from the east to the west end of Lake Ontario.

The real head of navigation on Lake Ontario was not Burlington Bay at the west end, but the mouth of the Niagara Gorge at Queenston. From here the first settlement made a rough road, following an Indian trail, to Chippawa Creek above the Niagara Falls, where navigation could be resumed. The distance was only 13 miles, but it involved a climb up the Niagara Escarpment of 300 feet. This road was progressively improved and became a most important artery of travel before the opening of the Welland Canal in 1832.

Perhaps the most famous road in British North America was the Cariboo Trail of British Columbia. It was constructed from Fort Yale, at the head of navigation on the Fraser River, to the gold fields of the interior, and the part that clung to the walls of the Fraser Canyon was a marvellous piece of road construction for its day. Plan and supervision were provided by a detachment of Royal Engineers, but most of the work was done by private contractors. The distance by road from Fort Yale to Barkerville, the final destination of the Trail, was 385 miles. It was soon crowded with freight wagons pulled by oxen, trains of pack mules, and even for a brief interval with camels. But the stage coaches were the popular form of transportation; driving day and night, they made the trip from Fort Yale to Barkerville in four days.

The Atlantic colonies had trunk roads from the early days of settlement. The important routes were from Halifax to Truro and from Annapolis Royal to Windsor. The most strategic, however, was the Temiscouata Trail, which linked Saint John, New Brunswick, with the St Lawrence Valley. It was also known as the Portage Road, because it provided an alternate route to the long sea voyage around Nova Scotia and up the Gulf and River of St Lawrence. In winter, when the great river was closed by ice, the 350-mile Temiscouata Trail was almost the only link between the Canadas and the Atlantic colonies. In 1813, six companies of the 104th Foot made the trip on snowshoes and sleighs, to reinforce the inadequate Canadian garrisons. The road followed the Saint John River to about the present boundary between New Brunswick and Quebec, then turned up the Madawaska River to Lake Temiscouata, and from here climbed over a narrow range of hills to the St Lawrence River at Rivière du Loup.

ROAD CONSTRUCTION

The first passages through the wilderness were footpaths and bridle-trails. Many were later expanded to a width that would permit passage of vehicles, but the main roads of colonial times were deliberately surveyed and cleared over new routes. First, the surveyor or pathmaster laid out the course and had it marked with slashes or 'blazes' on the tree trunks. Then came the axemen, who felled the trees along a strip usually 66 feet wide. The trunks were cut as close to the ground as possible, because at this stage there was no practical method of removing the stumps. The logs were piled by the side of the road, or used to fill swampy stretches. Many important roads remained in this condition for years. Usually, however, some crude ditching and grading were attempted, creating a dirt road, which was adequate in dry weather, but a muddy bog in spring or after a heavy rain.

A common answer to the need for an all-weather surface was the corduroy road, named somewhat ironically after the soft, corded fabric. It was made by laying logs, usually those obtained by the original clearing, transversely across the roadway. As no attempt was made to face the logs, and little effort to grade them by diameter, the resultant surface was a series of humps and hollows, over which the vehicles proceeded by jolts and pitches. Logs became displaced, rotted, or sunk into the mud, creating holes into which wheels descended with a crash, immobilizing the vehicle or even causing an upset. Many travellers in Canada, during the first half of the nineteenth century, recorded their unhappy recollections and even dangers on the corduroy road.

In Europe, many improvements in road building had been introduced in the late eighteenth century. The most famous of these was the macadam road, named after its inventor, the Scottish engineer John McAdam. This method of road building was to prepare a flat foundation of earth, and on this lay *crushed* stone, coarse grades below and finer above. Dust was added at the surface, to settle between the stone fragments and provide cohesion without rigidity. Some flexibility with good drainage were the secrets of success with the macadam road.

These roads were introduced to Canada in the 1830s. Lacking machinery to crush rock, and having to depend on expensive manual labour, the builders seldom used anything like as thick a layer of stone as was called for in the macadam design. Even so, such 'stone roads' were an immense improvement over the dirt and corduroy roads.

A peculiar Canadian type of road construction was introduced in the 1830s. This was the plank road. It was made by laying two or three rows of rectangular timbers lengthwise on the road bed, and nailing across them a continuous flooring of planks, three or four inches thick and a foot or more in width. As 16-foot planks were the lengths usually available, the plank road was only wide enough for one vehicle. So it had to have numerous turnoffs, or even a parallel dirt road alongside. Plank roads when new were smooth and dry, and provided comfortable transportation, but their upkeep was expensive, due to damage or rotting of the wood, and eventually this led to their abandonment as a method of road construction in the 1850s.

Funds for the construction of roads were provided from taxes, but in most settled areas a period of road work was one of the requirements of land owners. Some local roads were built by the voluntary efforts of the residents. In the 1820s, toll roads were introduced. These were operated by private companies, who undertook to build and maintain certain roads in exchange for the right to erect toll gates and to collect tolls. Such roads were

91 *Cheating the Toll*, from a painting by Cornelius Krieghoff, dated 1871

unpopular, not only because of the expense to the traveller, but also because the proprietors often skimped on the upkeep of the road. Krieghoff's well-known painting, *Cheating the Toll*, reflects the popular attitude towards this form of taxation.

Sooner or later the road builders encountered a stream to be crossed. Small streams ordinarily could be forded, but might become impassable in time of flood. Wider streams were crossed by ferry, some sort of barge that could be pulled across on cables, or rowed or poled. The bridge, however, was the obvious method of spanning a stream, and bridges were built from the earliest days of road construction. The Huron Road, built by the Canada Company from Guelph to Goderich, was unusual in that it was constructed in advance of settlement, and had many of its bridges installed at the same time that the road was built.

Early bridges were crude and showed little understanding of the stresses involved and the means of distributing them. In the usual construction a pair of logs or stringers were laid from one bank to the other, and to these the logs or planks of the deck were fastened. If the stream was too wide for a single span of logs, one or more piers were built on the stream bed, rectangular log cribs filled with gravel. Such piers made the bridge vulnerable to floods and particularly to ice jams.

More sophisticated frame bridges appeared when saw-mills made sawn lumber readily available. In this type of bridge the longitudinal beams on each side were reinforced by an upper frame of diagonal beams, which transferred the vertical stresses in the middle of the bridge to horizontal stresses against the abutments. Frequently these frame bridges were covered with board walls and roof, which kept out the snow in winter, and gave some protection against rotting of the timbers.

Masonry bridges were never numerous in Canada, as wood was so much easier to procure than stone, and skilled carpenters more readily available than experienced masons. Most of those that were built employed the Roman arch to distribute the weight on the span to the abutments and piers. Bridges of this sort were mostly built for railways, an excellent example being still in use at Trenton, Ontario.

When structural steel became available in the mid-nineteenth century, the so-called iron bridge was introduced. Most of these resembled the wooden-frame bridge, with an upper frame of girders to take up the stresses. For large structures the tubular iron beam was sometimes used, as in the case of the famous Victoria Bridge at Montreal, opened officially by Albert Edward, Prince of Wales, in 1860.

Another, very different, kind of construction was the suspension bridge, in which the vertical stresses of the span are taken up by heavy cables curving from towers at the ends. The famous suspension bridge across the Niagara Gorge below the falls was completed in 1855. It had an upper deck for railway tracks and a lower, closed-in passage for vehicles and pedestrians.

CONVEYANCES

Much travel, and even transportation, in colonial times was by walking and backpacking. Many a pioneer farmer carried his produce to mill or market on his back, and returned with flour or other provisions in the same manner. Government officials, doctors, and clergymen often used the saddle-horse, with ample saddle-bags for provisions or equipment.

In the Mountains of British Columbia the pack-horse or pack-mule was widely used to carry loads on trails too narrow and precipitous for vehicles. The pack-saddle is a simple device, with no seat, and the front and back corresponding to pommel and cantel, consisting of crossed pieces of wood, the ends projecting so as to provide attachments for load and rope. The pack of sacks or boxes was suspended from these projections by rope loops and secured in place by the 'hitch'. There were various kinds of hitches, but the best known was the 'diamond'. In using this, a doubled rope was thrown across the load from the two ends of the girth, then the free ends of the rope were doubled back along either end of the load and each interlaced at the middle with one of the central strands. When the ends of the rope were pulled, the central strands were drawn widely apart in a diamond shape, and this applied great pressure to the load. It was needed to prevent loosening of the hitch as the horse and its burden swung from side to side along the rough trail.

The commonest road vehicle in French Canada was the cart. This consisted of a box or frame mounted on a single axle, with two large wheels. It could be pulled by one horse, or by two horses in tandem, using a pair of shafts, or with a team of horses or oxen using a tongue. Some sort of rigid connection was needed, as part of the weight of load fell on the draught animal. Carts were good for handling heavy loads on rough roads, but having no springs they were very uncomfortable for passengers.

A special form of cart was used by the fur traders in the Fort Garry region, which became known as the Red River cart. It differed mainly from its eastern prototype in that no metal was used in its construction. The light frame was of poplar or pine and the axle and wheels of oak. All parts were held together with raw-hide strips, which were bound on while wet and allowed to dry and shrink. Sometimes the axle-hubs were lubricated with buffalo tallow, but this gathered the dust of the trail, causing rapid wear to the moving parts. The dry axles emitted a peculiar shriek as the cart moved, and this sound, magnified by numbers, signalled the progress of the métis brigade as it followed the buffalo herds. The single horse was harnessed to the shafts with raw-hide straps, and the Indian name for this material, 'shag-ganappie', came to mean anything that was improvised and of inferior quality. A later generation of western Canadians used the term 'hay-wire' in the same sense.

English Canada preferred the four-wheeled wagon. In this the two axles were joined together by a longitudinal beam called a reach, and the wagon box or frame sat on this 'running gear', held in place by four uprights. Springs made of steel strips might be introduced between the box and its supports. The front axle was made to swivel on a central pivot to permit turning corners. For the same reason the front wheels were usually smaller in

92 Farm wagon

diameter than the rear wheels. The front axle was attached to a
single shaft or 'tongue', the front end of which was suspended
from the harness of the two horses by means of a transverse bar
called the neck-yoke. This permitted control of direction, but the
pull was provided through leather straps called traces, which
extended from the shoulder harness to the whiffletree. The latter
was an arrangement of three wooden poles, the middle one being
pivoted at the base of the tongue, the other two being attached at
their middle each to one end of the middle pole. This left four free
ends, which were provided with hooks, to each of which one of the
traces was attached by a short length of chain.

A special type of vehicle appeared in Upper Canada with the
coming of the German-speaking settlers from Pennsylvania. This
was the Conestoga wagon, named for the town in Lancaster
County, Pennsylvania, where it was made. It was large, and
strongly built to survive the battering of rough frontier roads.
The most distinctive feature was the shape of the box, the bed of
which curved gracefully down, then up, from one end to the other.
The front and back walls of the box were not vertical, but were
inclined outward. The overall shape was that of a square-ended
boat, and that was the purpose of the design. With seams well
caulked, these boxes could breast the water of deep fords and

93 Conestoga wagon

keep their contents dry. More conspicuous, perhaps, was the canvas cover, which was supported on a series of widely curving hoops. This provided shelter for load and passengers in bad weather, and made the wagon possible sleeping quarters for overnight stops. In the early years of the nineteenth century hundreds of settlers made the trip from south-eastern Pennsylvania to the Niagara area, the Grand River Valley, and the district north-east of York (Toronto). The 'covered wagon' that achieved some fame much later in the settling of the American West had a canvas cover something like that of the Conestoga wagon, but the wagon box was of the conventional shape, with flat bed and vertical ends.

Other parts of British North America had their peculiar wagons. In Saint John, New Brunswick, the ships from the West Indies landed their puncheons, great barrels containing about 100 gallons of rum or molasses. These then had to be transported to warehouse or shop. In order to make loading a little easier, wagons were made with a short, heavy body, which was stepped down nearly to ground level in the space between the axles. It was not too difficult to tip a full puncheon into this depressed space, where it was secured with ropes for the trip. For some reason this peculiar vehicle was known as a sloven. It is said that when ships were being unloaded, the sloven drivers gathered their wagons around like taxis at a railway station today, and bid vigorously against each other for engagement.

As the road improved, passenger vehicles became more numerous. In Quebec, as with the cart, the two-wheeled calêche was the most popular. This was much simpler than the elegant vehicle of the same name that was used in France. However, they had in common a two-wheeled frame, a single seat for passengers, and a driver's seat perched over what would be the dash-board on a four-wheeled carriage. In the Canadian version the body was supported on two strong steel bands, sometimes coiled at one end, which served as springs.

In English-speaking settlements the corresponding vehicle was the buggy. It was small, and lightly constructed, but had four high wheels. The seat was single, as in the calêche, but there was a dash-board in front. The driver sat on the main seat, along with one or two passengers. The springs were steel straps, mounted transversely over the axles. There was usually a fabric and frame cover over the seat, widely open in front and capable of being folded back down in fine weather. Buggies were drawn by a single horse, in shafts, or a light team, using tongue and whiffletree.

A roomier vehicle called a surrey was similar to the buggy but longer and with a second seat installed in the rear. In this vehicle the top was usually a permanent fixture. From the surrey, it was no great transition to the more elegant carriage, provided with running-boards, splash-guards, and a pair of lanterns. Such a vehicle was for prosperous townspeople. For the average farmer, even the buggy was a luxury. He preferred a dual-purpose vehicle, such as a light wagon with a low box, to the sides of which one or two seats might be attached when required. Such vehicles became known in later years as democrats, perhaps an American allusion to their plebian function.

Another type of light vehicle of American origin was the buckboard. In this the bed was made of flexible boards, which were suspended at the ends over the axles but unsupported between. The springiness of the boards supplied the resilience usually provided by springs. Buckboards were used in place of buggies, but models with two or even three seats were common.

Winter was the season of travel in colonial Canada. Even the worst of roads became hard and smooth with frozen mud and a cover of snow and ice. The ice of frozen streams could be crossed without bridge or ferry, although not always without danger. In winter, farmers visited their friends and neighbours, or hauled their wheat or butchered pigs to market. All this was possible because sleighs could be substituted for wheeled vehicles. Almost every form of summer vehicle had its winter counterpart, differing little except in the use of runners instead of wheels. The two-wheeled cart was replaced by the jumper, a simple box or frame mounted on a pair of runners. Jumpers were usually pulled by a single horse in shafts, but a yoke of oxen might be used for heavy going.

The equivalent of the wagon, with four runners instead of wheels, and the front pair on a swivel, was simply called a sleigh. It was the standard freight carrier in winter, but lined with straw and provided with blankets and buffalo robes, it was often used to transport groups of people on social occasions.

The winter equivalent of the calêche was the carriole, but there were other differences aside from the replacement of the wheels by two long runners. The carriole had high sides, which almost wrapped around the passengers and protected them from cold wind and flying snow. Some carrioles had a seat for the driver in front, as in the calêche, but more often they were designed to be driven by the owner himself, seated comfortably behind the dash-board with his companions. Carrioles were drawn either by a single horse in shafts or by a team pulling with traces only. They varied from elegant vehicles to little more than boxed-in jumpers.

In the English colonies the carriole was replaced by the cutter. The runners were slender, and gracefully curved up in front. The body was supported high above the runners by a series of narrow struts. This enabled the vehicle to cut through two or three feet of snow. The sides of the body were not as high as those of the carriole, but the dash-board rose in a graceful S-curve, to provide protection against the snow and slush scattered by the horse's hoofs. Elegant carriage bodies were made so as to be transferable from wheeled running gear to a set of sleigh runners. It was not necessary to have two sets of runners, as with the freight sleigh. The weight of the carriage and passengers was light enough to allow the horses to skid the runners around turns.

With almost any type of winter vehicle on runners it was customary to embellish the horse's harness with leather straps bearing rows of bells. These were brass spheres, slotted and perforated, with a metal ball inside. The sound of the bells served

94 *The Overturned Sleigh*, from a painting by John B. Wilkinson, showing a jumper and cutter

95 Sleigh running-gear on which a wagon box could be set

as a warning to pedestrians or other vehicles on the narrow roads, but they became traditionally associated with winter travel.

STAGE COACHES

When main roads became usable, or at least passable, at all times of the year, the operation of scheduled transportation became possible. Stage lines, so highly developed in eighteenth-century Europe, did not appear in Canada until the nineteenth century. They required not only adequate roads, but suitable stopping places at intervals of about 15 miles, where the team of horses could be replaced, and the travellers might obtain food and rest.

By the 1830s, regular stage-coach runs were providing dependable service between Halifax and Kentville, Quebec and Montreal, Montreal and Toronto. The stage coach evolved from a converted wagon to the traditional closed body with a door and windows on each side, and two or three seats within for the passengers. The driver sat on a seat at the front of the roof. Behind him was a rack for light luggage, and a leather-covered compartment ('boot') at the rear for heavy cases. The coach body was not supported on springs. Instead, it was slung from the axle-frames on two very heavy leather straps, which allowed the body to sway alarmingly without providing much resilience against bumps. In winter the coach body was transferred from the wheeled running gear to a frame with two pairs of runners, like the farmer's sleigh. Now, with the roads hardened and smoothed by ice, stage-coach travel was much more comfortable and reliable, in spite of the cold weather.

Coaches were drawn by two teams of horses, the rear or 'wagon' team being hitched to the whiffletree and tongue in the usual manner, and the lead team to a second whiffletree attached to the front end of the tongue. A rein was attached to the outside ring of each horse's bit; the inner or adjacent reins were linked by a cross-strap. The driver not only had to manage the four reins, but also to flourish a long whip with which, if he were skilful, he could flick each of the horses as required, or crack it in the air with a pistol-like report. The horses were driven as fast as the condition and grade of the road would allow. On smooth, straight stretches, and especially on coming down a hill into a valley, they were driven at full gallop, for momentum was needed to get up the other side. The brakes were applied through a foot-operated lever, and were none too effective. It was the skill of the driver, combined with well-trained horses in good condition, that made the stage-coach trip swift and comparatively safe. Most of the accidents that did occur were breakdowns of the vehicles, due to the severe beating that they took on the primitive roads. Often the passengers were called upon to help with the repair of a wheel or the extrication of the coach from a mud hole.

The stage stations, about 15 miles apart, were usually inns. On approaching one of these the driver sounded his horn, which was the signal for the hostlers to bring out the fresh harnessed teams, to be hitched in replacement as soon as the coach drove in. Passengers disembarked for a brief rest or perhaps a meal. Then

96 Stage coach

97 Reconstructed staging inn, 'Halfway House', as it was in 1854. Black Creek
Pioneer Village, Ontario

the horn was sounded, the passengers boarded the coach again, and with a cracking of the whip, a rattle of wheels, and a clatter of hoofs, the stage coach was off on the next section of its run. The daily arrival and departure at a station was a brief interval of excitement in the routine of a small community.

Some stage lines enjoyed years of successful operation and good repute, as a result of excellent organization and first-class equipment. Expenses were often met in part by government contracts to carry the mail. One of the best-known lines was that of William Weller, which operated between Toronto and Montreal. Mr Weller seems to have resembled his Dickensian namesake, in being not only a skilful coachman, but also a picturesque character with a flair for humorous speech.

RAILWAYS
The practice of running wheeled vehicles on rails made of wooden planks or wood faced with iron strips, goes back to the early years of the eighteenth century. This kind of transportation was used mainly in mines, and propulsion of the cart was by horse or man power. It was not until 1825 that a wheeled vehicle, propelled by a steam engine, was driven along rails. This was the achievement of George Stephenson of England. In 1830 he and his colleagues inaugurated the first scheduled railway service. The first steam railway in America was the Baltimore and Ohio, which began operations in 1831. In the United States the new form of transportation was called the railroad, whereas in Canada the British term railway was, and still is, preferred.

Rail transportation in Canada began with the Champlain and St Lawrence Railway in 1836. This was designed to by-pass the Chambly Rapids on the Richelieu River and provide a short cut from Lake Champlain to Montreal. It is said that the engine imported from England could not be made to work until a 'Yankee' expert was brought in, and prescribed 'plenty of wood and water'. The rails were of wood faced with iron, and were very rough and unstable.

In 1853 the first railway in Canada West (Ontario) began operation out of Toronto. This was the Ontario, Simcoe, and Huron Railway, later renamed the Northern Railway. Intended to link Lake Ontario with Lake Simcoe and Georgian Bay, the first run could go only as far as Aurora, a distance of 25 miles. In 1854 the line was completed to Collingwood, finally justifying the name. And so the old North West Fur Company route was brought back into use in a new way by the steam railway. Another early railway designed to provide an alternative to water travel was the Cobourg and Peterborough Railway, which connected Lake Ontario at Cobourg with the Trent Waterway and the prosperous district of Coborne, of which the town of Peterborough was the centre. This line, only about 30 miles in length, had a long series of misfortunes and setbacks. The major difficulties lay in the crossing of Rice Lake, a combined causeway and bridge three miles long, which was unable to withstand the pressure of winter ice and storms. Later this line was used for the transportation of iron ore from Marmora, but when this industry declined the railway fell into disuse and was eventually abandoned.

The most famous Canadian railway before Confederation was the Grand Trunk. It was built both to tap American trade and to link Montreal and Toronto. The railway opened in sections, beginning in 1855. The first through train from Toronto to Montreal reached that city on 27 October 1856. By 1858 the line had been pushed westward through Guelph, London, and Sarnia to link up with the railways of Michigan. Completion of the Victoria Bridge across the St Lawrence River at Montreal in 1859 permitted the Grand Trunk Railway to extend into the eastern townships of Quebec, and eventually to link with the Intercolonial Railway to the Atlantic colonies of New Brunswick and Nova Scotia.

Like most early Canadian railways, the Grand Trunk had prolonged financial problems, many of which were the result of bad judgment. An example was the decision, contrary to expert advice, to use a width between rails of 5 feet 6 inches instead of the standard American gauge of 4 feet 8 inches. The latter curious dimension originated because it was the width between the wheels of stage coaches. Nevertheless it was the generally accepted gauge in North America, and the choice of a wider gauge in Canada made it impossible to interchange rolling stock or pass trains between that country and the United States. The expensive conversion to the narrower standard gauge was not made until the period 1872–74.

First railway in the Atlantic provinces was the Nova Scotia Railway, which was completed from Halifax to Truro and Windsor in 1858, and to Pictou in 1867. The Halifax-Truro section later became part of the Intercolonial Railway, which linked Nova Scotia and New Brunswick to Quebec in 1876.

With the exception of the very early Champlain and St Lawrence Railway, all of the pioneer railways in Canada began in the 1850s. Hence the equipment was much the same, being imported from England and the United States at first, and later manufactured in Canada to the same designs. The locomotives were small by later standards. There were two pairs of large driver wheels, connected by drive rods to the pistons of the steam cylinders. Under the cylinders was the truck, pivoted to negotiate curves, and mounting two pairs of much smaller truck wheels. A large, triangular, grating-like device projected prominently forward from the front of the truck to deflect obstructions on the way. This was popularly known as the cow-catcher, which suggests what the commonest kind of obstruction was, but railwaymen called it the pilot. The main part of the locomotive was the large cylindrical boiler, with the fire-box at the rear. The door of the fire-box was inside the cab. Here, the 'engineer' operated the controls, and the fireman kept the flames roaring by throwing in split sections of logs. For these early locomotives were all wood-burners, and piles of these log sections were carried in the tender, a separate car behind, which also had a tank for the boiler water.

One of the most conspicuous features of the wood-burning locomotive was the smoke-stack, which was tall and spread to a wide opening at the top. This housed a screen designed to prevent the escape of sparks with the smoke, which might have started fires along the right of way. Sometimes these screens became clogged with cinders, so that the draught of the fire was diminished, and then one of the crew had to climb forward and tap these obstructions loose with a stick. Other conspicuous features of the upper profile were the headlight—an oil lantern with a reflecting mirror—the valves to control the steam pressure, and the bell. The steam whistle was mounted on the rear valve. Its deep tone was a familiar background to the steam railway. Various combinations of long and short blasts were used to communicate with the crew or the surroundings. The best known was the road-crossing signal, two long, a short, and a long.

Patrons of the early railways rode in passenger cars which were provided with a row of double seats on either side of the middle aisle. In the wall at the end of each seat was a small, double-paned window. Ventilation was provided by louvre-like openings in the roof. Oil lamps were suspended above the aisle. At each end of the car was a small platform with steps. Hitching one car to another was done by means of links and pins, which had to be loose enough for free movement, but which as a result produced disconcerting jolts on starting and stopping. On one of the platforms was the brake wheel, which had to be turned to set the brake shoes. When it was necessary to stop the train unexpectedly, the engineer 'whistled down the brakes' with a series of short blasts, whereupon the brakeman tightened the brake wheel. As this had to be done for each car, the response to an emergency was not very fast, even with an experienced crew, and derailments often occurred that might have been avoided if the train could have been stopped more quickly.

Cars for transporting luggage and light freight were like the passenger cars but with only a few windows and with sliding doors on the sides for loading and unloading. Heavy freight was carried in 'box-cars', with large rectangular bodies and sliding doors. Unlike the European goods van, the box-car had pivoted trucks, each with two pairs of wheels.

Railway travel in colonial times was an ordeal. The rails were light and not solidly joined, so that the inevitable gaps between caused a sequence of minor but irritating jolts. The cars were dirty from the soot of the engine, which could be kept out only by cutting down on ventilation. In winter, some heat was provided by a wood-burning stove at one end. The seats were hard and cramping. Most travel was by day; the sleeping-car was not invented until 1864. In addition to these discomforts, there was the ever-present danger of wreck by derailment or collision.

In spite of these unpleasant aspects, the experience of rolling along at a speed of 20 or 30 miles an hour on a relatively smooth road, with a reasonable expectation of arriving on schedule, was such a contrast to stage-coach travel in confined space, swaying from side to side, crashing into mud holes, and arriving bruised and weary at some uncertain hour, that there was no doubt as to the advantages of the new mode of travel. The luxury of one generation had become the hardship of the next.

14

Education

The education of the young under the French régime was almost exclusively the responsibility of the Church. The Ursuline Nuns who came to Quebec in 1639, under Mother Marie de l'Incarnation, took as one of their duties the training of Indian girls. This consisted mainly of teaching household crafts and inculcating religious practices. As the population of French settlers grew, a need was felt for education of the boys, especially for the priesthood. Bishop Laval, who came to Canada in 1659, started the Séminaire du Québec in 1663. From this nucleus developed the classical college so characteristic of education in French Canada. Subjects taught, such as Latin, philosophy, and rhetoric, were those required for entrance to the priesthood, although only a part of the student body went on to that life. Meanwhile, elementary education of both boys and girls was the task of the priests and nuns, and many schools were associated with convents. The system was making some progress towards universal education by the time of the British conquest (1760), but subsequently fell into disuse, and after two generations or more of educational deprivation, the habitant class became largely illiterate.

THE BRITISH RÉGIME
The Loyalists who emigrated from the former American colonies to British territory in 1783, and later, were accustomed to community schools, open to all children. Those who wished to continue this tradition met some opposition from the authorities, who held the European ideas of the time that education was for the children of the élite, as determined by social rank or financial means. This approach had indirect support from some groups of settlers, such as the Pennsylvania Germans, who urged that their

children were needed at home to help with farm work, and that they should not be obliged to pay for the education of other people's children. In contrast were the Scottish settlers, who wanted education for all.

Bishop John Strachan was bitterly criticized, in his day and later, for his efforts to maintain the domination of the Church of England and of the governor and council. But he did make a start with universal education in Upper Canada. Through his influence the Grammar School Act of 1807 was passed, permitting the setting up of publicly-supported secondary schools. It is said that he started at the wrong end, but the trend was extended to the elementary schools by the Common School Act of 1816. This might have happened earlier but Upper Canada had gone through a three-year war in the interval.

In the meantime, local schools had been started, usually by the resident clergyman. The first of these was at Cataraqui (Kingston) in 1785. The most prestigious of all Canadian private schools, Upper Canada College, was founded at York (Toronto) in 1829. Universal education became government policy in this province in 1846. Nevertheless, the schools of Upper Canada, as of other parts of British North America, were woefully primitive by modern standards. The buildings were small, with only one room. They were usually log cabins, but sometimes were frame buildings of crude construction. In earlier times, heat was provided by a fireplace at the end, but when stoves became generally available, there was one in the middle of the room. Firewood was provided by the community in the form of log sections, but these had to be split for use by the teacher or the older boys. The pupils sat on benches along three of the walls, and the teacher had his desk on the fourth side. Desks for the students were a relatively late innovation. Usually the teacher's aids were only a blackboard and a map of the world. The pupils worked with slates, on which they scratched their lessons with a thin rod, also of slate. The use of pen, ink, and paper was reserved for the senior members of the class. Ink came in crockery bottles, from which the ink wells were filled. Probably some apothecary in a nearby town made it by mixing iron sulphate with an infusion of oak galls (tannic acid). Pens were made from feather quills, usually the wing feathers of a goose. These were trimmed, then heated or steamed to make them hard. The tip was cut off obliquely and the interior cleaned out. Final operation was making a fine longitudinal slit in the tip. Pen points wore out quickly, and were resharpened with a small pocket knife, which therefore came to be called a penknife. Almost anyone who could read and write and who was a British subject was eligible to teach. Many of these teachers were Americans, who had taken the oath of allegiance, but whose inclination was to glorify everything American. Because the discipline required to control teenage farm boys had to be strict, country teachers were almost always men. Sometimes they were retired soldiers. Fights between students had to be prevented, and it was not unusual for the teacher himself to have to subdue the leader of the rowdies before discipline could be established. Whipping with cane or strap was normal punishment, and was accepted by pupil and parents as the privilege of the teacher. Women taught mostly in town schools, especially those for the training of young ladies. In the country, the teacher 'boarded around', that is, lived with one of the local families for two or three months, then moved on to another. Salary, outside of the provision of room and board, was meagre, and often paid in produce, which the teacher himself might have to sell to get his money.

Under such primitive conditions, and with such ill-trained teachers, the curriculum was very limited. Primary emphasis went to reading and writing. After memorizing the alphabet, pupils practised copying the letters on their slates, and on pronouncing the words. Great emphasis was placed on spelling, which was learned by repetition. Arithmetic was called ciphering, and included addition, subtraction, multiplication, and division, which were based on memorized tables. The 'rule of three' was the mathematical high point in the curriculum. If the teacher were sufficiently qualified, English grammar was taught to the senior pupils.

Just getting to school was an important part of the educational process in rural communities. Distance from home to school was usually several miles. A large family might send the children off in a wagon or buggy, the horse being driven by the oldest boy. In winter the sleigh or cutter was used. Boys commonly rode to school on horseback, usually without a saddle. But mostly the children just walked to school and back, a distance of two or three miles not being considered excessive. They carried their lunches in knapsacks or pails, and supplemented their cold meat and dry bread with water from the school well.

Tradition has built an aura of sentiment about the memory of the 'little red school house', which was customarily white or unpainted. But the records show that it was frequently an unhappy place for both teacher and pupils, and that the education obtained there was inadequate even for the requirements of those days. The children who went on to become lawyers or doctors usually attained the necessary level of basic education by self-instruction. Prosperous town families, of course, could send their children to private schools, thereby conferring a great advantage on them in later life. Making good education universally available was the work of dedicated leaders. Upper Canada was the testing ground, where Egerton Ryerson laid the foundation of a universal and compulsory system, in spite of opposition at the top from Bishop Strachan, and at the bottom from conservative rural communities. Ryerson was a Methodist clergyman and Superintendent of Provincial Education from 1844 to 1875. He set up a system of state-supervised but locally-supported schools, incorporating the best elements of European and American practice so that at the time of Confederation (1867), the school system of Canada West, renamed Ontario, was the standard on which those of the other English-speaking provinces were based. Ryerson's counterpart in Canada East (Quebec) was Jean Baptiste Meilleur, in Nova Scotia, Theodore Rand, and in British Columbia, John Jessop.

The British American provinces had a special problem in education, due to the close association of schools with the religious denominations. To the Roman Catholics it was fundamental that there be religious instruction in the elementary schools. The Church of England also favoured this, but being a less cohesive establishment, was forced to go along with the Protestant denominations. So a dual system grew up of non-Catholic (public) schools and Catholic (separate) schools, which was legalized in Canada West in 1841. In French Canada the situtation was reversed, as the great majority of citizens were Catholics. Polarization here took place between the French-language Catholic schools and the English-language schools, with the English-speaking Catholics and the French-speaking non-Catholics finding it difficult to fit into the system. But the English-language schools were never restricted in any way, which made more acceptable the establishment of Catholic separate schools in other parts of Canada. In Newfoundland, all schools were operated by religious denominations, with the support of public funds.

In a country where elementary schooling was obtained with difficulty, and secondary education was available only to children of the more prosperous families, it was a long time before there were many universities. One of the first was McGill University, created in 1813 by a bequest from the Montreal merchant James McGill. For years it existed more on paper than in fact, its earliest activity being the medical school that it absorbed in 1838. Its real history dates from 1855, when the Nova Scotia geologist George William Dawson took over as Principal, and vitalized the teaching of the arts and sciences. The leading French-language university in Quebec was Laval University, founded as such in 1852, but tracing its origin to the Séminaire de Québec set up by Bishop Laval in 1663. Dalhousie University, in Halifax, Nova Scotia, was created in 1818, but like McGill did not become active until much later (1838). The University of Toronto was begun by Bishop Strachan as King's College in 1827, and was under the direct control of the Church of England. When the University of Toronto was formally established in 1850 there was a bitter struggle between Bishop Strachan, representing those who wished to retain sectarian control, and John Langton, the Provincial Auditor, one of the majority who favoured a non-sectarian university. The victory of the latter, and the creation of the University of Toronto as an independent centre of learning, led Bishop Strachan to disassociate himself from it and to found Trinity College in 1851. Meanwhile, Queen's College had been set up in Kingston in 1841 by the Presbyterian Church, but open to all denominations. In the same year the Methodists expanded their Upper Canada Academy in Cobourg to form Victoria College which subsequently became affiliated to the University of Toronto.

15

Social Activities

In the most primitive societies men have felt the need to participate in some form of group activity, such as a feast, a dance, or an athletic contest. The early settlers of Canada had the same urge. In spite of harsh weather, inadequate food and housing, and the threat of hostilities, the French colonists found some means of relaxation. The first and one of the most famous was Champlain's Order of Good Cheer, which he organized among the small band of Frenchmen at Port Royal, in the winters of 1606 and 1607. This was a kind of feasting club, in which each member took his turn at organizing the table and the entertainment.

No such happy association relieved the troubles of the first inhabitants of Quebec, which Champlain founded in 1608. The responsibility of organizing and defending an outpost 3,000 miles from home did not leave much time for conviviality. Later, as Quebec and its satellite settlements of Montreal and Trois Rivières became more populous, the inhabitants sought some form of relaxation. Their choice was governed by the fact that men were in the majority over women in the population, a condition that persisted until near the end of the seventeenth century. As a result, men sought their amusements in the inns and wine shops, where they drank, sang, or gambled at cards.

Growth of family life in New France brought a greater interest in amusements at home. Neighbouring families were invited for the evening. Besides convivial conversation there was singing, dancing, and modest feasting. This kind of entertainment was carried over into the British period.

The English-speaking settlers who came to the British colonies after the American Revolution brought their ideas of entertainment, which in many cases, as with the French, featured parties and dances. But large elements among the newcomers, such as the

Methodists, the Quakers, and the Mennonites, looked on such activities as sinful, and sought their social intercourse mainly in events connected with their church.

Of all the occasions for festivity in both French and English Canada, the wedding was the most popular. Even among the strict sects it was a happy occasion that called for feasting. With the French Canadians it was a major celebration, at which the families of the couple provided abundant food and drink, and the facilities for prolonged dancing. However, if such a celebration were not provided, or if the bridegroom were unpopular, or much older than the bride, the couple might be treated to the French custom of the *charivari*. Hence this was originally a spiteful affair. The men of the community, more or less disguised, surrounded the marital house after dark, beat pans, blew horns, and shouted insults. They might be bought off by a distribution of liquor.

The custom was carried over into English Canada, although the name became changed to shivaree. Gradually it took on a more good-natured character, like the throwing of rice, and the tying of old shoes to the bridal carriage.

98 *Canadian Wedding*, from a painting by James Duncan (1806–1882)

MUSIC

At any informal gathering in French Canada, the singing of folk-songs was likely to be one of the activities. Many of these traditional songs were from the south of France, and are said to have been brought to Canada by the regiments sent to assist in the defence against the Indians and the British. The fact that many of these soldiers were billeted in homes during the winter months, suggests how the songs were introduced. In the Atlantic colonies, too, folk-singing was a popular form of domestic entertainment. Musical instruments were few, and players even fewer, so the singing was without accompaniment, and the melody simple and plaintive. It was the story told by the words that interested the listeners.

Even when musical instruments such as violins and flutes became common during the eighteenth century, they were used mainly for providing music for dances. In the Scottish settlements, bagpipes were brought by the earliest arrivals, but they too were for dancing or for marching. Instruments such as the concertina, the guitar, the dulcimer, the harmonium or reed organ, and the pipe organ, were introduced in the nineteenth century, mostly from England or the United States, and provided accompaniment for both popular and religious singing.

Military bands were brought to Canada by British regiments garrisoned here. Towards the middle of the nineteenth century, community bands became popular, and performed for celebrations and parades. The musicians were volunteers, but the leader was often an experienced professional, who received a small salary for his services.

DANCING

Of all the forms of social entertainment in colonial times, the dance was by far the most popular, especially among the French Canadians, where it flourished in spite of the Church's disapproval. A wedding, a visit of relatives, or just the urge for some fun, could lead to a night of revelry that might go on until dawn. In French Canada, dances were held in the house, often in the kitchen, which was usually the largest room. If the house of the host were not spacious enough, he might borrow that of his neighbour for the occasion.

In English Canada, most of the houses were too small, and dances were held in the barn, perhaps at the conclusion of a corn-husking or an apple-paring bee. The school house, if large enough, might be used as the ballroom. As more pretentious inns were built in the nineteenth century, they included a large upstairs room for dances, which could serve at other times as emergency lodging.

Music for the dances was usually provided by a violinist or 'fiddler', who might play with his instrument pushed against his waist rather than tucked under his chin. In English Canada the violin was often augmented by a concertina or a second violin. The pieces were simple, repetitive melodies in lively time, but the rhythms were often complex. Principal qualifications for members of the 'orchestra' was the stamina to keep playing for hours, with little intermission.

There were various groups of dances, each with its particular tunes. Among the French Canadians the minuet was the most popular. In this dance, several couples form two lines, the men on one side, the women on the other. In time to the music the lines approach and separate, and the couples execute special steps and circle each other, hand in hand. As performed in the grand balls of the upper classes, the minuet was the slow and stately dance of eighteenth-century Europe, but at the dances of the petit bourgeois, and the habitant, a more vigorous and unorganized version was performed, with improvised steps and individual variations.

Similar dances were popular among the Loyalists and other immigrants from the United States. The best known of these was the Virginia Reel, said to be similar to the English country dance called Sir Roger de Coverley. In this, in addition to performing minuet-like steps, the partners promenade individually between the lines.

The quadrille, almost as popular in French Canada as the minuet, was performed in groups of two couples, with various circular and 'in-and-out' movements. Here again the Loyalists brought their version, the square dance. In this, the groups or 'squares' were made up of four couples, and moved under the direction of a 'caller', who announced the various movements in a kind of chant in rhythm with the music. Square dancing was vigorous and exciting, and was quickly adopted by the enthusiastic French Canadians. Another group of nineteenth-century dances were the round dances, performed by a number of couples in a single circle. The best-known version, the schottische, was relatively slow and stately, but there were more vigorous versions. The Scottish settlers brought with them a long tradition of

99 *Circular Dance of the Canadians*, from *Travels through the Canadas*, by G. Heriot, 1807. The women wear typical Empire-style dresses, while some of the men wear breeches and others the new trousers

dancing, including characteristic reels as well as the famous solo dances by men. The Irish immigrants also brought reels, and the well-known jig, in which the dancing is done without arm movements.

GAMES

Next to dancing, the French Canadian colonists enjoyed most their various games of cards. Playing cards were in good supply in New France, and on occasions when coinage was scarce, were endorsed and circulated as paper money. Men played cards for money, often for high stakes. The favourite games were picquet and quadrille, both members of the whist family. Picquet is a two-handed game, played with a reduced deck. Players score not only by the tricks taken, but also by the value of their hand after a draw. Scoring is complicated. Quadrille is a four-handed form of whist, with complicated rules for determining trump.

Whist was the fashionable card game with the English-speaking colonists, that is, those to whom card playing was not a moral lapse. It is played by four persons, each opposite pair being partners. The trump suit is determined by turning up the last card dealt. Scoring is based on the number of tricks taken and the number of 'honours' (court cards in the trump suit) in the tricks taken. Modern bridge was derived from whist by introducing bidding of the number of tricks each player thinks he can take, the trump suit being that of the successful bidder.

Two card games that are widely played today were introduced to pre-Confederation Canada. One of these is cribbage, a two- or four-handed game in which the score is kept on a perforated board. This is an English game, introduced by the Loyalists in the late eighteenth century. Poker is a gambling game, in which various combinations of cards have particular values, but most of the interest in this game is in the betting which takes place after the deal and during the play. This is traditionally a game of the south-eastern United States, and reached Canada about the middle of the nineteenth century.

Checkers was a popular game among the French colonists, being played with pieces that differed in shape rather than colour. Billiards was also popular. Chess, apparently, was played very little until the arrival of the English-speaking settlers.

The inhabitants of French Canada seem to have had few organized outdoor games. Lacrosse, an Indian invention, was occasionally played by the French. Racing was popular, including sleigh and snowshoe racing, as well as canoe racing and the usual horse racing. Curling was introduced soon after the establishment of British rule. Tradition has it that it was played on the ice of the St Lawrence River by Scottish soldiers during Murray's defence of Quebec, in the winter of 1759–60.

The English settlers brought bowls, cricket, and football (soccer). Athletic contests were common, often between teams representing rival communities. Wrestling was the most popular trial, with more liberal rules than would be tolerated today. Foot races and tugs-of-war were also popular. Scottish settlers favoured contests involving strength, such as hammer-throwing and shot-putting.

About the middle of the nineteenth century the American game of baseball began to displace cricket. Baseball is derived from the English game of rounders, but is played with a pole-shaped bat, and a diamond-shaped field, with four bases instead of two. Another late arrival was Rugby football, from which Canadian and American football were derived. These variants, it seems, did not originate with deliberate intent, but rather from a misunderstanding of the English game.

Much outdoor amusement was less formally organized.

Hunting and fishing, grim necessities for many a frontier settler, were fascinating sports for English immigrants. Horse racing was an incidental adjunct to celebrations, or perhaps just organized to settle a rivalry, and betting was informal. Target-shooting for prizes could be another part of a local sports day. In winter, snow-shoeing parties were the thing, but usually restricted to men, at least as participants. Winter drives in cutter or carriole, or by large groups in hay-stuffed farm sleighs, could include the young women as well as the men. The game of ice hockey, so generally identified with Canada today, was a deliberate merging of the old English game of field hockey with the sport of skating. Tradition, much disputed, has it first played in 1855, by members of the Royal Canadian Regiment stationed at Kingston.

BEES

Of all social gatherings the most characteristically Canadian was the bee. It was brought from the United States by the Loyalists, but soon became well established in all the British colonies including Lower Canada. Previous mention has been made of the barn-raising bee, the apple-paring bee, and the quilting bee. Other occasions for bees were land clearing, fence-building, or the taking in of the harvest of a sick or deceased neighbour. The responsibility of the person who 'called' the bee was to provide plenty of food and whiskey. Although these outdoor bees were concerned with men's work, the women of the households prepared the quantities of food that were devoured by the male participants. Bees were often criticized by magistrates and by advocates of temperance. The excessive consumption of liquor frequently led to quarrels and fights, and sometimes to injuries or deaths.

Women had their own special bees, which not only helped members of the community, but also gave an opportunity for friends and neighbours to meet, and to exchange news, recipes, and domestic lore. The quilting bee was the commonest, but there were sewing bees and spinning bees. The German communities had social gatherings for making sausage and apple butter. Favourites with the young people were the apple-paring bees and the corn-husking bees, because the boys and girls participated together. In the corn-husking bee, each lad who husked a red ear of corn had the privilege of kissing his young lady partner. Such bees concluded with a supper and a dance, the latter being the highlight of the occasion.

PUBLIC EVENTS

Parades and public ceremonies were very popular in the British American colonies. In the French period they had been mostly associated with religious celebrations, such as the annual festival of St John The Baptist (St Jean Baptiste) on 24 June. Under the British régime the birthday of George III, 4 June, was the national holiday long after the death of that monarch. It was not superseded until 1837, when Queen Victoria ascended the throne and her birthday, May 24, became the day of national celebration.

'The twenty-fourth of May is the Queen's birthday.
If we don't get a holiday we'll all run away.'

These royal birthdays were the occasions not only of patriotic celebrations, but also of the annual muster of the militia. The day began with assembling of the local company. Writers both contemporary and subsequent have had a lot of fun describing the disorganized shambles that was called a drill. No doubt their accounts are true, but they missed the real purpose of the gathering. Each militiaman had a chance to see his officers as well as his fellow soldiers and to get some feeling of belonging to a military body, however rudimentary. When the test came in 1837, and a group of embittered rebels threatened British rule, the militia of Upper Canada organized quickly, and by the third day were in Toronto in overwhelming numbers. Had the vacillating governor summoned them when the threat first arose, they would have intimidated the rebels into submission by the sheer threat of their numbers. Again in 1838, in the second uprising in Lower Canada, it was the militia of Huntingdon and Ormstown who defeated the rebels in the two decisive fights at Odelltown.

The epoch-making tour of British North America by H.R.H. Albert Edward, Prince of Wales, in 1860 was the occasion for a series of celebrations that accompanied the royal itinerary. There were parades and balls, presentations and dedications. A great wave of patriotism swept across the colonies, which bore fruit in the resolute defence of Canada in 1866 and 1870 against the Fenian invaders, and created a sense of unity which led to Confederation of the provinces in 1867.

16

From Colonies to Nation

The official end of the colonial period in Canadian history, or at least the beginning of the end, occurred on 1 July 1867, with the proclamation of the British North America Act. This legislation by the Parliament of Westminster united Nova Scotia, New Brunswick, Canada East (Quebec), and Canada West (Ontario) as the Dominion of Canada, a federation of four provinces, each with its own continuing legislature, but with a central government for the whole. Manitoba became the fifth province in 1870, and British Columbia, after much debate, joined in 1871. Prince Edward Island, where the idea of Confederation started in 1864, held out until 1873. The gap between Manitoba and British Columbia was closed in 1905 with the creation of two new provinces, Saskatchewan and Alberta. Newfoundland, the oldest British colony, remained aloof in pride and suspicion until 1949.

If the political development of Canada was slow and by stages, alterations in the Canadian way of life brought about by Confederation were insignificant at first. The major changes had already occurred. Loss of free trade with the United States in 1866, a seeming disaster, was turning Canadian interests toward local manufacture, but the shift was gradual. The technological advances of the 1840s and 1850s, such as the steam railway, the Bessemer steel furnace, and the kerosene lamp, had no equivalents in the 1860s and 1870s. It was not until 1880 that the next great invention, the electric light, began to appear in factory and home.

The event that stabilized the new nation and at the same time reorientated Canadian life was the completion of the Canadian Pacific Railway in 1885. This, together with the Intercolonial Railway of 1876, gave reality to the Dominion's motto, 'From Sea to Sea'. At the same time it opened thousands of square miles of new land to a wave of settlement. At first this came from the eastern provinces, but soon the sources included the United States and Europe. This was a second era of colonization, with the prairies taking the place of early nineteenth-century Canada, and the provinces of Ontario and Quebec substituting for Britain and the United States as the sources of manufactured goods and a market for agricultural products.

The pioneer farmer of the western plains went through much the same stages of development as had his eastern precursor. There was little or no clearing to be done, but there were isolation, primitive living conditions, sweltering summers and frigid winters, crop failures, and even a war (the North-West Rebellion of 1885). It was like a repeat performance of the 1783–1850 settlement of Ontario and Quebec. But technological advances were catching up with the pioneer. Branch railways and better roads improved communication. Steam tractors and complex farm machinery displaced horse-powered devices. Improved varieties of wheat decreased the losses from frost and rust. Electrical power and telephones spread out from the cities. The internal-combustion engine, in automobile and tractor, provided mobility and efficiency. By the second decade of the twentieth century the new colonial period was over. The prairie farmer and townsman were living the same sort of life, and enjoying the same amenities, as their eastern counterparts. Only in the north was there still a field for the explorer and the pioneer.

SELECT BIBLIOGRAPHY

Arthur, E. R., *The early buildings of Ontario*, 1938
Asselin, E. D., *A French-Canadian cookbook*, 1968
Bealer, A. W., *The art of blacksmithing*, 1969
Boorman, Sylvia, *Wild plums in brandy. A cookery book of wild foods in Canada*, 1962
Bouchard, Georges, *Other days, other ways*, 1928
Brett, K. B., *Women's costume in early Ontario*, 1965
Futcher, W. M., *The great north road to the Cariboo*, 1938
Gillespy, William, *The Canadian housewife's manual of cookery*, 1861
Gowans, Alan, *Building Canada. An architectural history of Canadian life*, 1966
Guillet, E. C., *Early life in Upper Canada*, 1933, 1963
Guillet, E. C., *The great migration. The Atlantic crossing by sailing-ship since 1700*, 1937, 1963
Guillet, E. C., *The pioneer farmer and backwoodsman*, 1963
Gullet, D. W., *A history of dentistry in Canada*, 1971
Haight, Canniff, *Country life in Canada fifty years ago*, 1885
Hamil, F. C., *Lake Erie baron; the story of Colonel Thomas Talbot*, 1955
Harvey, D. C., *The colonization of Canada*, 1936
Heagerty, J. J., *The romance of medicine in Canada*, 1940
Henry, L. J. and Paterson, G., *Pioneer days in Ontario*, 1938
Howell, W. B., *Medicine in Canada*, 1933
Innis, M. Q., *Mrs. Simcoe's diary*, 1965
Jameson, A. B., *Winter studies and summer rambles in Canada*, 1838, 1965
Jeffereys, C. W., *The picture gallery of Canadian history*, 1942
Jenness, Diamond, *The Indians of Canada*, 1932
Johnston, J. F. W., *Notes on North America agricultural, economical and social*, 1851
Jones, R. L., *History of agriculture in Ontario, 1630–1880*, 1946
Langton, Anne, *A gentlewoman in Upper Canada*, 1950
Langton, W. A., *Early days in Upper Canada*, 1926
Lizars, R. and K. M., *In the days of the Canada Company*, 1896
MacLaren, G. E. G., *Antique furniture by Nova Scotia craftsmen*, 1961
Macrae, Marion and Adamson, Anthony, *The ancestral home. Domestic architecture of Upper Canada*, 1963

McInnis, Edgar, *Canada. A political and social history*, 1947, 1969

Minhinnick, Jeanne, *At home in Upper Canada*, 1970

Moodie, Susanna, *Life in the clearings*, 1853, 1959

Moodie, Susanna, *Roughing it in the bush*, 1852, 1962

Palardy, Jean, *The early furniture of French Canada*, 1963

Peirce, J. H., *Fire on the hearth   The evolution and romance of the heating stove*, 1951

Reaman, G. E., *A history of agriculture in Ontario*, 1970

Reaman, G. E., *The trail of the black walnut*, 1957

Russell, C. P., *Firearms, traps & tools of the Mountain Men*, 1967

Russell, L. S., *A heritage of light.   Lamps and lighting in the early Canadian home*, 1968

Savard, Pierre, *Paysans et ouvriers québécois d'autrefois*, 1968

Séguin, R.-L., *Le civilization traditionel de l' 'habitant' aux XVIIe et XVIII siècles: fonds matériel*, 1967

Séguin, R.-L., *L'equipment de la ferme canadienne aux XVIIe et XVIIIe siècles*, 1959

Skelton, Isabel, *The backwoodswoman*, 1924

Stevens, Gerald, *Canadian glass* c. *1825–1925*, 1967

Storck, John and Teague, W. D., *Flour for Man's bread.   A history of milling*, 1952

Strickland, Samuel, *Twenty-seven years in Canada West or The experiences of an early settler*, 1853, 1970

Thompson, Samuel, *Reminiscences of a Canadian pioneer, for the last fifty years, 1833–1882*, 1884, 1968

Thomson, D. W., *Men and meridians*, vol. 1, 1966

Traill, C. P., *The backwoods of Canada.   Being letters from the wife of an emigrant officer*, 1836

Traill, C. P., *The Canadian settler's guide*, 1855, 1969

Traquair, Ramsay, *The old architecture of Quebec*, 1947

Vincent, Rodolphe, *Nôtre costume civil et religieux*, n.d.

Wackerman, A. E., Hagerstein, W. D. and Michell, A. S., *Harvesting timber crops*, 1949

Wright, Lawrence, *Home fires burning.   The history of domestic heating and cooking*, 1964

INDEX

INDEX

INDEX

205

INDEX

INDEX